101 Really Important Things You Already Know, But Keep Forgetting

OTHER NOTABLE BOOKS BY ERNIE J. ZELINSKI

How to Retire Happy, Wild, and Free: Retirement Wisdom That You Won't Get from Your Financial Advisor

The Joy of Not Working: A Book for the Retired, Unemployed, and Overworked

Real Success Without a Real Job: The Career Book for People Too Smart to Work in Corporations

101

Really Important Things You Already Know, But Keep Forgetting

Ernie J. Zelinski

TEN SPEED PRESS
Berkeley | Toronto

Published by Visions International Publishing in association
  with Ten Speed Press.

Ten Speed Press
P.O. Box 7123
Berkeley, California 94707
www.tenspeed.com

FOREIGN EDITIONS:
Published in Spanish by Amat Editorial, Barcelona
Published in Russian by Gayatri Publishing, Moscow
Published in French by Stanké International, Montreal
Published in Chinese traditional characters by Yuan-Liou
  Publishing, Taipei
Published in Chinese simplified characters by CITIC
  Publishing House, Beijing
Published in Korean by Mulpure Publishing, Seoul
Published in English in Malaysia by TrueWealth Publishing,
  Kelana Jaya

Library of Congress Cataloguing-in-Publication Data
Zelinski, Ernie J. (Ernie John), 1949–
101 really important things you already know, but keep
forgetting : how to make your life more enjoyable day-by-day,
year-by-year / Ernie J. Zelinski.
p. cm.
  ISBN 978-1-58008-882-4 (alk. paper)
1. Conduct of life. I. Title. II. Title: One hundred one really
important things you already know, but keep forgetting. III.
Title: One hundred and one really important things you
already know, but keep forgetting.
  BJ1581.2.Z44 2007
  170'.44--dc22

                                     2007026613

Printed and bound in Canada
  1 2 3 4 5 6 7 8 9 10 — 12 11 10 09 08 07

Dedicated to My Wonderful Mother
Violet Zelinski
(Waselyna Gordychuk)
August 5, 1921 – February 8, 2007

Who passed away while I was completing this book — and meant
so much to her friends, her relatives, and me for so many years.
We all love you and miss you dearly.

Contents

PREFACE

Have you ever noticed how history has a habit of repeating itself? Many situations in which you find yourself today are likely similar to ones you have experienced sometime in the past. The other participants, as well as the stage, may have changed along the way — the deep-laid plot and intriguing drama are all too familiar, however. Through each of the scenes, you get to learn several important concepts of living that you have already learned several times — but keep forgetting.

You may have first encountered some of these life principles when you were in grade school. Nevertheless, you have had to relearn them from time to time, in some cases too many times to count. Keep in mind that it is all too easy to carry the baggage of your youth into your later years. You don't want to be sixty or seventy years old and saying, "Any day now, I am going to get my act together and stop making this same costly mistake over and over again."

This is the reason that this book focuses on many of those life lessons that most of us have already learned — but for some mysterious reason keep consigning to oblivion. Sometimes it's not all that mysterious; it's just a case of our acting out of emotion instead of consulting our intellect. Knowing which situations to avoid and which principles to follow is important for a full, rewarding, happy, and enlightened life. Indeed, failure to abide by these life lessons can drastically affect our personal and vocational success.

In large measure this book is autobiographical. Even while writing it, I occasionally found myself promptly violating one of the principles about which I had just written. In one case, it was somewhat embarrassing when it cost me some money and my pride. I thought of the graffiti writer who claimed, "I learn from my mistakes — I can make the same mistake with greater ease the second time around."

To be sure, experience increases our knowledge, but it doesn't necessarily decrease the number of our mistakes. Best-selling author Richard Bach wrote, "Learning is finding out what you already know. Doing is demonstrating that you know it." It follows that knowledge can be called wisdom when we start using it and benefiting from it. Intelligent action, in other words, is required to transform valuable knowledge into wisdom.

You will notice that much of the content in this book is just plain common sense. Oliver Wendell Holmes Sr. once said, "We all need an education in the obvious." In the same vein, a Latin proverb states that common sense is not all that common. What's more, philosophers tell us common sense in an unusual amount leads to wisdom.

I hope that this book will also give you an insight or two instead of just reminding you of what you already know. There may indeed be a few life lessons that you previously haven't learned. Martin Vanbee warned us, "Learn from the mistakes of others — you can't live long enough to make them all yourself."

After reading this book you may finally get the message about some of life's important principles so that you don't have to relearn them the hard way. Perish the thought of never violating all the lessons in this book, however. There will always be moments of weakness in your life during which you repeat some mistake you have made several times before.

Your goal should be to minimize the number of important lessons you keep forgetting and the number of times you forget them. Try to read this book with an open heart and an open mind. Apply the principles that resonate with you and discard those that don't.

Whenever working on a new project, I always keep in mind the words of Thomas Carlyle: "The best effect of any book is that it excites the reader to self-activity." My wish is that the life lessons in this book infect you with the inspiration, motivation, and commitment needed to attain your dream of having a full, relaxed, satisfying, and happy life.

1

You Don't Have to Know the Meaning of Life to Enjoy It Fully

Ever since human beings developed the abilities to reason and explore, they have searched for the big secret. Philosophers, scientists, and theologians alike have been searching for the undisputable answer to the question: "What is the meaning of life?" This perplexing question has resulted in a wide range of conclusions and arguments, including scientific theories, authoritative dogma, philosophical conjecture, and spiritual explanations.

As a matter of course "What is the meaning of life?" is the most profound question most individuals ask themselves at some point during their lives. The question in itself is open to various interpretations: Why are we here? Who are we? Where did we come from? What is the purpose of life? Will we experience life after death?

To get the upper hand on everyone else, you yourself may be determined to get to the bottom of this mystery called life — not even sure how much longer you can hang on if you don't find it. Plain and simple, it is unlikely that you will succeed. All things considered, there likely will never be an answer. Many individuals with greater talent and knowledge than you and me have come up empty-handed. You will find that the deeper you go, the more the mystery will deepen.

You may even decide to go traveling around the world in search of the magical answer to life. The further the better, you think — maybe even ashrams in Colorado or the Himalaya Mountains in south-central Asia. Once you get there, you will make an interesting discovery: The only answers and enlightenment you get to experience in ashrams in Colorado or mountaintops in India are the answers and enlightenment with which you arrived.

This doesn't mean that you shouldn't learn more about the world. It's rewarding to explore and discover the fascinating aspects of life. By all means, keep looking to improve your understanding of many things around you. It's best to let some of the more profound things remain mysterious, however.

Sometimes too much understanding of something beautiful — such as the scientific explanation for what causes the Northern Lights to be visible in the night skies of northern U.S.A., Europe, Russia, and Canada — makes it less beautiful.

In the same vein, having the absolute understanding of life — if there ever will be one — would undoubtedly make life less enjoyable. Richard Bach in *Illusions* wrote, "Learn what the magician knows and it's not magic anymore." Not to mention that desperately contemplating the meaning of life can lead to stress, ulcers, high blood pressure, and a lack of success. At the extreme, people frantically searching for the meaning of life have been known to commit suicide.

Even if you discover the absolute meaning of life, you may realize that it doesn't really make any difference to the quality of your existence anyway. Your answer may be that ultimately life is pretty meaningless, that we are all insignificant grains of dust in the grand cosmic scheme of things, that we are all leading random lives, that our existence doesn't affect anything or anyone.

George Carlin may have actually found a far better answer to the meaning of life. Now don't get too excited, because his answer isn't as profound as you may anticipate. Carlin once said that the ultimate meaning of life is "to find a place to put all your stuff." This, indeed, is as good of an answer as any other.

In short, if you want to reduce the existential angst in your life, give up your self-adopted role as chief investigator of what makes this universe rock. No amount of brooding about the meaning of life can take the place of going out there and enjoying all it has to offer. The mistake most people make about pursuing the meaning of life is searching for the answer instead of living it. The search in itself may give some people meaning but it seldom brings a smile to their faces.

How right Rita Mae Brown was when she said, "I finally figured out the only reason to be alive is to enjoy it." When you learn to enjoy all that life has to offer, there is no need to understand it. Viewed in this way, the meaning of life is to live fully — to enjoy the ride, in other words.

2
Life Is Tough — But Then Again, Compared to What?

Unfortunately, when you arrived on this planet, no one gave you an instruction book on how to deal with life. In your early teens you were expecting life to be one big party once you got your act together as an adult. What a surprise! A few years after reaching adulthood and having to deal with the real world, you came to the realization that life is difficult. In this regard American philosopher George Santayana surmised, "Life is not a spectacle or a feast; it is a predicament."

Regardless of your age, if you expect living to be easier down the road, forget it. What may come as a surprise is that life is difficult for everyone. Your life won't be free of difficulty no matter how talented and how rich you become. Truth be told, everyone experiences stress and pain to a certain degree.

Illness, natural disasters, accidents, death, and other negative events are inevitable. None of us is immune. The successful of this world take for granted that the world is a hard place. Carl Jung, the well-known Swiss psychiatrist, felt that unpleasant experiences help us find personal and spiritual wholeness. "Man needs difficulties," said Jung. "They are necessary for health."

As a matter of course the world throws curves at all of us throughout our lives. In the event you ever find that everything is coming your way, you will probably be on a one-way street going the wrong way. You may go through a stretch in your existence when so many things are going right that you start believing that nothing of consequence could go wrong. As is to be expected, when you get on a roll, you will start thinking that you finally understand how life works.

Alas, just when you are convinced that you are under divine guidance, something will happen to burst your bubble. Disaster will strike when you least expect it. Most of the time, however, things appear a lot worse than they are. Nothing very good lasts a long time — neither does anything very bad. How many times have disasters become blessings in disguise?

Everything changes sooner or later. The good becomes bad and the bad becomes good. Profits turn into losses and losses turn into profits. Approval may turn into disapproval and disapproval may turn into approval. Mistakes and setbacks add up to success. Then success leads to failure. This is life. It is never too late to start again.

As tough as things get sometimes, there are several ways to make life more alluring — things as simple as looking at the bright side of things. "When life's problems seem overwhelming," syndicated columnist Ann Landers told us, "look around and see what other people are coping with. You may consider yourself fortunate." It also helps to realize that nothing is as serious as it first appears. Today's crisis makes tomorrow's interesting story.

American novelist Kathleen Norris has a formula for making your existence a lot less difficult: "Life is easier to take than you think; all that is necessary is to accept the impossible, do without the indispensable, and bear the intolerable." Indeed, the more you can hold up to the tests of the real world, the more you can achieve. The key is to put your mind at ease and rely on your inner strength to handle the difficult times confidently and successfully.

All told, life is a learning process and the school of hard knocks is a great teacher. Pleasure and comfort don't build character — adversity does! Once you acquire your Master's in Adversity, you will be prepared for the worst of situations. As Clare Boothe Luce, an American playwright and public official, once emphasized, "There are no hopeless situations; there are only people who have grown hopeless about them."

Life can be relatively difficult or it can be relatively easy. Our material environment has nothing to do with how difficult it is. What matters is how we react to our environment. Paradoxically, surrendering to the fact that life isn't always easy will make it a lot easier. Whenever you feel that life is overwhelming you, just subject yourself to this mind-altering question: "Yes, life is tough — but then again, compared to what?"

3

Life's a Breeze When You Work As Hard at Simplifying It As You Do at Complicating It

Yes, life is tough. But life can be a lot easier when we keep things simple. Surprisingly, you would think that human beings would work at simplifying their lives, but the opposite is true. Given a choice between a simple way and a complicated way of doing things, most people will choose the complicated. Preposterous as it may seem, some of us will even spend time inventing a complex way when none is immediately available.

No question, we do not need to make our lives more difficult. Given the opportunity, plenty of other individuals in this world will gladly do this for us. Life's unexpected events will also put our creativity to the ultimate test without our having to create our own special difficulties.

The words you are least likely to hear from anyone in American society today are "My life is way too simple." Fact is, most individuals make their lives way too complicated and wonder why they have so many big headaches and major problems.

Why people make their lives unnecessarily complicated is a mystery to philosophers and psychiatrists alike. I am just as amazed at how far out of their way most people will go to find a myriad of methods to complicate their personal and business lives. They waste a lot of money, time, and energy on pursuing things that bring them nothing in return. They may also hang around people who will do them absolutely no good.

All of us, to some extent or another, practice the philosophy of my good friend Todd Lorentz, who stated, "Just living in this world is a psychotic pursuit." At some point in our lives we all have the tendency to make our lives unbelievably complex and depressing. We manage to do this with our material possessions, work-related activities, relationships, family affairs, thoughts, and emotions. As is to be expected, we are unable to achieve as much as we would like because we invite too many physical and mental distractions into our lives.

Yet life's a breeze when we work as hard at simplifying it as we do at complicating it. If you are the type of person who can't leave home without four-fifths of your personal possessions, it's time to lighten up a little on your journey through life. Without delay, get rid of the burdens that have become a drain on your time, space, money, and energy. Do something today to make your life less complicated.

To enjoy life to the fullest, you must periodically identify the things that complicate your existence. This applies to both the personal and career aspects of your life. Make a list of the things that no longer serve a worthwhile purpose in your world. Ask your friends to add to this with suggestions as to how you can simplify things. Your friends may see much opportunity where you may see none.

Sure, you didn't invent complexity. You do your absolute best to perfect it at times, however, don't you? Keep in mind that making the simple complex doesn't take ingenuity. Making the complex simple — now, that's ingenuity!

Apply common sense and you won't have much difficulty in simplifying your existence. This is about getting the excess baggage out of your life. "No man can swim ashore," observed the Roman philosopher and dramatist Seneca, "and take his baggage with him." To be sure, life is much easier if you don't carry excess baggage.

Whatever your destination, you can't afford to carry excess baggage for too long. On trains and airlines, it will cost you extra money. On the trip called life, it will cost you much more than money. At best, you won't succeed in achieving your goals as quickly as you otherwise would. At worst, you will never succeed in attaining your goals. Not only will this deprive you of satisfaction and happiness, but it could cost you your sanity in the end.

4
Happiness Doesn't Care How You Get There

In his work *Nicomachean Ethics* written in 350 B.C., Greek philosopher Aristotle claimed that happiness is the only thing that humans desire for its own sake. People seek riches, not for the sake of being rich, but to be happy. Likewise, individuals desire fame, not for the sake of being famous, but because they believe fame will bring them happiness. According to Aristotle, the highest good for us is happiness, and that is why we desire and seek it.

As an experience and a subject, happiness has been pursued and commented on extensively since the dawn of history. This reflects the universal importance that humans have placed, and still place, on happiness. Of course, spiritual leaders, philosophers, psychologists, and economists have different notions on the nature of happiness and how to attain it.

One thing is certain: If you are to be happy and awaken to the beauty of the world around you, you must put your life in synch with your deepest values and beliefs. You must pursue what you truly want out of life and not what others want you to pursue. This is not an easy thing to do, particularly in modern Western society, where we are subject to so many outside influences.

For instance, it is all too easy to get too intoxicated with the dream of what conventional success is going to do for your happiness. Yet conventional success and happiness are two entirely different things. Conventional success — a big house, a beach cabin, two or three fancy cars, an extremely attractive spouse, and a high-powered job — hardly serves any other purpose than to make life extremely difficult for most people.

Erich Fromm in his book *Escape from Freedom* wrote, "Modern man lives under the illusion that he knows what he wants, while he actually wants what he is supposed to want." Indeed, in today's consumer society advertisers and the media dictate what people are supposed to want. Many people consume this programming greedily instead of stopping to question what will truly make them happy. After all, it is much easier to try to fit in with the majority than to question what the majority is doing.

Yet following the majority as they look for happiness in all the wrong places is insane. Understand that happiness doesn't care how you get there. It doesn't care how hard you work. Nor does it care whether you wear designer clothes or how fancy your car is or how many possessions you have. Moreover, happiness doesn't care how beautiful, talented, or intelligent you are.

Perhaps by now you are thinking that these are just crazy assumptions. On the contrary, there is much scholarly evidence to support these statements. Research by psychologists indicates that the things that most people assume would make life better — money, fame, status, beauty, or social prominence — over the long run don't seem to matter all that much, if at all.

For example, one research paper reported that physical attractiveness has at most a very marginal effect on how content people are in life. Another study concluded individuals may be pleased for a month or two after a big lottery win, but there is no relationship between the money and ultimate happiness a year later. Still other research has shown that social standing, age, intelligence, and education have no effect on true happiness.

How happy you are depends on whether you are willing to be happy. Happiness will elude you as long as you are thinking and doing what's wrong for you. And it will come easily when you are thinking and doing what's right for you. Above all, ensure that you don't get conned into believing happiness is what someone else deems it to be.

You can rest assured that you will never attain true happiness if you wait for destiny or others to show you the way. Whether you are black or white, male or female, illiterate or highly educated, single or married, tall or short, or rich or poor, happiness leaves you in charge of whether you get there. The Dalai Lama told us, "Happiness is not something ready-made that Buddha can give you. It comes from your own actions." Take his advice and run with it. It will be extremely valuable to you on your journey through life.

5

Slow Down in Your Pursuit of Happiness and It's More Likely to Catch Up with You

In modern life, as in Greek tragedies, should we be astonished that many successful people aren't happy people? In case you haven't noticed, conventional success is much easier to attain than happiness. There are hundreds of thousands of neurotics who are successful — but there are no happy ones!

So how do you create happiness if you are successful and not happy? First, don't desperately pursue happiness. Happiness, it seems, doesn't like people who are desperate for it. Slow down in your pursuit of happiness and it's more likely to catch up with you. The more you search for happiness, through success or otherwise, the more it will seem to elude you. You can't achieve happiness by buying it or continually striving to achieve it.

Paradoxically, if your primary goal in life is to be happy, happiness will always be beyond your grasp. "The search for happiness," Eric Hoffer declared, "is one of the chief sources of unhappiness." Victor Frankel echoed those remarks when he wrote, "It is the very pursuit of happiness that thwarts happiness." And Edith Wharton agreed by stating, "If only we'd stop trying to be happy we'd have a pretty good time."

Instead of pursuing happiness, start living life according to the way things are instead of the way they should be. Much unhappiness is caused by the belief that life should be different from what it actually is. Accepting reality for what it is will liberate you from the imprisonment of what ought to be.

Don't be dismayed when the world hasn't brought you what you want. For many of the things that you have been denied the universe has brought you something better. It is your duty to discover what it is. Surprisingly, a happy life isn't the absence of unhappiness. Unhappiness will sneak into your life whether you want it or not. So will happiness. What you choose to do with either is up to you.

When happiness forgets about you, see what treasures you can find in your unhappiness. It won't be long before happiness remembers who you are, and sneaks back into your life again. Keep in mind that ten times as many good things happen to you as bad things. This is a good reason to spend ten times as much time ranting and raving about the wonder of life as you do complaining about it.

In your search for Shangri-la, don't overlook the possibility that paradise may be where you are right now. Everyone seems to want to be somewhere they aren't. Choose to be where you are right now and you will be happier than 90 percent of humankind.

Just as important, why waste so much time, energy, and money trying to buy the biggest house that your credit rating will allow? Truth be told, a small house can hold as much happiness as a large one. Sometimes, in fact, it will hold even more!

If you want to be happier, try going with the flow of life a little more. Let things happen naturally instead of always trying to make things happen. It's always easier to ride a horse in the direction it's going. In other words, be the source of happiness instead of looking for it. You don't have to pursue happiness if that is where you are coming from.

All told, happiness is a mode of traveling and not the destination. Happiness is a product of achieving goals, but not a goal in itself. Zen masters tell us that we corrupt the beauty of living by making happiness the goal. They say happiness is the practice of living in the moment; it's in everything we do. Learn how to live and to be happy one day at a time — and you will have mastered how to live happily ever after.

6

Predict Your Failures and You Will Become a Highly Successful Prophet

Most individuals expect that they can't accomplish anything of value in their lives — and they are seldom disappointed. The sad thing is they could make a big difference in this world if they didn't anticipate failure. "There isn't a person anywhere," asserted Henry Ford, "who isn't capable of doing more than he thinks he can."

Even the most gifted individuals — whether plumbers, poets, or pediatricians — will not accomplish much in this world, however, unless they free themselves from their self-imposed limitations. Confidence is everything when it comes to achieving success. Lack of faith in their own abilities is the main reason that most people don't come close to achieving their full potential. Self-doubt is much more prevalent than you may think. Everyone in this world, in fact, harbors self-doubt to some degree.

Like virtually everyone else in this world, you can accomplish more than you think you can. Most of your limitations are in your mind. The danger is that your false self-doubts can become real. Negative expectations bring about negative results. When you keep saying that things won't work out for you, you will get to be right about it. To look at this another way, predict your failures and you will become a highly successful prophet with an impressive track record.

It is important that you ignore any self-talk about why you can't accomplish something significant. Just as important, you must ignore other people who are just too willing to talk you out of trying something challenging. When you have faith in your abilities, it matters little when others say that your biggest goals cannot be achieved. In fact, if you have a winning attitude, you will be motivated even more to accomplish your goals when someone declares that these goals are unattainable. You will also discover the incredible satisfaction that comes from doing what others say you aren't capable of doing.

We all want to leave a mark on this world. We want to know that our life matters, that we make a difference somehow. So don't let your past failures hold you back. It's easy to let failure go to your head. If you have recently been experiencing obscurity, low self-esteem, unhappiness, or frustration, you have likely been doing something wrong.

Don't buy into the sentimental notion that success is an absurd, erratic thing attainable only by a few of the extremely talented. You have to break out of the rut and find some mountain to climb. "Argue for your limitations," warned Richard Bach, "and sure enough they are yours." You shouldn't settle for less than you are capable of attaining. Why settle for average when your talents — combined with motivation and effort — can put you far above average?

Whether it's making new friends or having a more fulfilling career, a dream not acted upon will remain just a dream. The strongest single factor in attaining any one of your dreams is self-esteem — believing you have talent and creativity, believing you deserve your dream, and believing that it is possible for you to attain the dream.

All things considered, the greatest failure is the person who doesn't try. When you spot an opportunity, you must be willing to do your best to capitalize on it. Give yourself permission to try and give yourself permission to fail. Failure will bring out your ignorance. Celebrate both your failure and your ignorance, because if you do, you will become wiser. And don't forget to give yourself permission to succeed. With success, you will become even wiser.

Roman poet Virgil concluded, "They can because they think they can." You must convince yourself that your limits are smaller and fewer than the imaginary ones you have been subjecting yourself to. Just getting by when you can do much better is no way to spend the rest of your life. There comes a time when you must get your act together and show the world and yourself what you can do.

7

The Pain of Unfulfilled Dreams Can Be the Worst Ache You Will Ever Experience

Many — perhaps most — people on their deathbeds reflect upon their lives with deep regrets. Ashley Montagu articulated this so well: "The deepest personal defeat suffered by human beings is constituted by the difference between what one was capable of becoming and what one has in fact become." If you are getting no satisfaction in your life, you undoubtedly know that the ache of unfulfilled dreams can be the worst pain you will ever experience.

If you experiment with a rat by consistently placing cheese in the third of several tunnels, the rat will eventually figure out the cheese is always in the third tunnel. The rat will go directly to the third tunnel without looking in other tunnels. Start putting the cheese in the sixth tunnel and the rat will keep on going to the third tunnel. Sooner or later, however, the rat will realize there is no cheese in the third tunnel; the rat will now start looking in the other tunnels until it discovers the cheese is in the sixth tunnel. As a matter of course the rat will now consistently show up in the tunnel with the cheese.

The difference between rats and human beings is that the majority of human beings will remain in a tunnel when there is no cheese in it. Weird — no doubt — but true. Most humans get themselves into traps from which they never escape. Clearly, it's pretty hard to get the cheese when one is caught in a trap that has no cheese left — or had no cheese in it in the first place. Needless to say, "cheese" here is a metaphor for happiness, satisfaction, and creative fulfillment that come from pursuing and attaining one's dreams.

Somewhat tragic is the large number — at least tens of millions — of stupendously intelligent, well-educated, highly trained, and extraordinarily skilled people in North America who have yet to experience any measurable success in their lives. These unhappy and disheartened people didn't follow through on their plans or pursue their dreams. Instead, they chose the best-paying job available and have remained in careers they don't enjoy. The problem is that after forty or fifty years of boredom, they are still in the same tunnel, without any cheese, wondering when the plots in their life stories will take a turn for the better.

On the other hand, there are individuals who are living their dreams. Dreams often do come true for many people, but only for those who focus and work on them. To be totally playing the game of life, you must have dreams toward which you are working. According to Richard Bach, "You are never given a wish without also being given the power to make it true — you may have to work for it however."

Clearly, you will never get satisfaction from the important things that you intended to do — but never got around to doing. Whether it's fame, fortune, romance, or adventure that is part of your dreams, you must go for it. If you are not getting satisfaction in your life, you must rearrange it. Otherwise, you are going to keep getting out of life what you have been getting.

What important things do you dream about most? There are probably several ambitions that you want to fulfill. Now is the time to explore your dreams and wildest fantasies to give you some clues as to what you should be pursuing in your life. You must identify the things that mean the most to you and then make them the focus of your existence. If you can't make your dreams happen where you are today, you must go somewhere else where you can make them happen.

Statistics provide overwhelming evidence that you are going to die — unfortunately, it could be sooner than later. Start doing those important things in life as soon as possible because you may not get as many chances as you are hoping for. Careful planning and sustained effort will go a long way toward achieving those dreams.

8

If You Want to Be a Star, It's Best Not to Bother with Other Things

Given the choice between pursuing a dream career and continuing a life of grindstone existence, most people opt for the grindstone existence. They tolerate abusive bosses, lousy working conditions, and boring, dead-end jobs simply because finding a better job takes time and energy. Moreover, pursuing a career dream requires change and risk-taking. Most people find it easier to stay with the familiar, even if the familiar offers extreme boredom and drudgery.

If you aren't pursuing your career dreams today, you are setting yourself up for much disappointment and many regrets later in life. Not having followed their career dreams is usually one of the biggest regrets people have later in life. It may surprise you, or even pain you, to find out that many people, after having attained fame and fortune, regret having devoted all their life energy to getting there.

Take, for example, George Soros, the famous currency speculator. Using his financial savvy, Soros amassed a fortune that has been estimated by *Forbes* to be over $8.5 billion. Yet he claims he would trade it all for a chance to have achieved his dream career. Being a philosopher — not making money — has always been his real passion.

The fascinating aspect of this is that the experience of George Soros is not uncommon. Countless people have worked hard, accumulated a substantial amount of money, and concluded that it wasn't worth it. They realized that with less money, they would only have given up things they didn't want or need anyway. What's more, they realized that they would have enjoyed themselves more along the way had they worked at something they enjoy.

You probably have dreams that you want to pursue and skills and talents that you would like to utilize somewhere in your work. You may have suppressed these skills and talents for years and years because you have become too obsessed with being successful in the traditional sense of the word.

This means making as much money as possible, in the shortest period of time.

Perhaps you realize that you can have a more meaningful, more fulfilling, and happier existence only if you make important changes in your life. All along, however, you have put off making a change because you are waiting for the perfect moment, with the right conditions. Clearly, there is no perfect moment. Waiting for things to get better will ensure that they don't get better.

To wish your life away in anticipation of living some long-awaited dream sometime in the distant future is to do yourself a great disservice. That future may never come — and in the event that it doesn't, you will never get satisfaction from the things that you intended to accomplish. Clearly, whether your vocational dreams include fame, creative accomplishment, or adventure, today is the time to start working toward those dreams.

You may have worked yourself up the ladder from nurse to the head administrator of New York's biggest hospital, for example, only to realize that you would rather live in a loft in SoHo and make a living as an artist. Alternatively, you may be working sixteen hours a day repairing safety helmets for an environmental corporation in northern Canada when deep down you want to be like your writer friends who are part of the Starbucks' laptop-and-cappuccino crowd. Whatever you think intuitively that you should be doing, you should give it some serious consideration and explore the possibilities.

Your work should be the principal expression for your mind and creative talent. You can put your purpose, talents, character, and dreams into a career in many ways if you use your imagination. Many options and opportunities await you, provided you look for them. Only you can determine what you specifically want, however, and only you can put yourself in the right direction toward getting it. In the words of American poet Walt Whitman, "Not I — not anyone else — can travel that road for you. You must travel it for yourself."

When choosing a new career, you must make every effort possible to select one that is right for you. "Do not put your spoon into the pot that doesn't boil for you," advises a Romanian proverb. Your pot will boil for you when your career allows you to pursue some important purpose that can make a difference in this world. A proper career should also allow you to utilize the special talents that you want to use. To really work for you, your career should be compatible with your character and the lifestyle you would like to lead.

Career dreams do come true for people, but only for self-confident individuals who constantly focus and work on them. Look around, and you will see many individuals living their vocational dreams. People have turned their hobbies into part-time businesses that have eventually become multimillion-dollar businesses. Others have given up careers for which they have been highly educated to pursue careers for which they had no education. Despite this disadvantage, they have been able to turn their dreams into realities and create abundance in their lives.

Long ago, you may have decided that your heart's desire was to be a criminal lawyer, for example, but now you realize that you really need something with a little more meaning. The ideal is to always work at something that makes a difference, to do the things you enjoy, and to use your most cherished talents.

It is never too late for a career change — the best time to pursue your dream career is twenty years ago and today. Whatever you would like to do, you must set in motion the forces that will get you there. The longer you put off pursuing your dream of a fulfilling career, the more time becomes your enemy. Time will steal your vocational dreams if you keep waiting for the right moment. You can always create more money — but you can never create more time.

Years from now, as you reflect upon your life, you don't want to regret not having earned your living by singing, designing software, working with children, building things with your hands, traveling to new cities, or inspiring others to new heights. It may hurt a little to realize that you have only dreamed about the interesting life filled with spontaneity and creativity. It will probably hurt a lot, in fact. Clearly, it's not what you become — but what you don't become that will hurt most in the end.

9
Do the Difficult and Uncomfortable If You Would Like an Easy and Comfortable Life

As we discussed earlier, life is tough. Luckily, there is a way to make the game of life much easier. You are about to be reminded about (or introduced to) an awesome, paradoxical life principle. It is called The Easy Rule of Life.

Following The Easy Rule of Life can get you from Loserville to Success City in record time. You may also want to call this principle The Easy Rule of Success. Once you master it, success will come relatively easy — much easier than it came before you mastered this rule.

The Easy Rule of Life tells us that when we always do the easy and comfortable, life turns out difficult and uncomfortable. When we do the difficult and uncomfortable, however, life turns out easy and comfortable. Think about it carefully, and you will see how this rule applies to your life.

Indeed, the principle that we must do the difficult and uncomfortable to experience true satisfaction and well-being influences every area of our lives, including work, financial gain, raising children, friendship, love, health, fitness, and retirement. Taking the easy and comfortable way — sitting at home and watching a lot of no-brainer programs on television — will put you on a dead-end street. Long-term satisfaction can only be attained by undertaking the challenging activities that are at times difficult and frustrating. We must pay the price with time, effort, and frustration in completing these activities.

In particular, think about how this awesome, paradoxical life principle applies to attaining anything related to success. To be sure, to have a lot of success in your life will not always be easy — you may have to do a lot of difficult and uncomfortable things. But once you attain this success, life will be much easier and much more comfortable. What's more, life will be much more satisfying because you have accomplished something extraordinary.

The Easy Rule of Life tells you that each day you should be doing something difficult and uncomfortable. If you have always wanted to write a book, for instance, but have resisted doing so, you are in the majority.

Apparently 81 percent of Americans think they should write a book — but only 2 percent have completed a manuscript.

This is one of the reasons that American novelist John Updike said, "Writers may be disreputable, incorrigible, early to decay or late to bloom, but they dare to go it alone." If you want to join the small minority of creative individuals that has completed a manuscript, you should force yourself to write for at least an hour or two each day. You must, in fact, go it alone. This may continue to be difficult and uncomfortable for a long time but eventually you will have the book completed.

Alas, most people would rather be comfortable than do whatever it takes to be successful. Be different from the masses — be willing to be uncomfortable! If you want to become a professional speaker, but would be scared half to death to speak in front of more than two people, then choose to be terribly uncomfortable. Make your first speech in front of one hundred people. Just as telling, be willing to do your first speech wrong, but at least do it. You will feel great because you will know that you have done your best.

If you want to be truly alive and experience a sense of achievement and satisfaction, you have to concentrate on doing many difficult and uncomfortable things — not just one. It's difficult and uncomfortable to be highly organized; it's difficult and uncomfortable to pay attention to the important things in life; it's difficult and uncomfortable to save money; and it's difficult and uncomfortable to keep agreements. Regardless of how joyless these things are, give up your comfort zones and start doing them.

It's all too easy to wring your hands and whine about the lack of opportunity in today's world. It's much harder and more uncomfortable to acknowledge that there is a lot of opportunity, spot it, and capitalize on it. If you are not doing something comfortless and risky every day, you are stagnating as a human being. There are probably a hundred different areas in your life in which you are taking the easy and comfortable way at this time.

Most people subscribe to the theory that difficulty is a good reason for not doing something. On the contrary, the idea that something is difficult is a good reason for doing it. Every extraordinary achievement was once considered not only difficult, but impossible by the experts. Yet this did not stop the people who pulled off these achievements. Think Edison! Think Gandhi! Think Mandela!

True greatness is not determined by status, power, and possessions. The foundation of greatness is good character, comprising such things as risk-taking, individuality, courage, and overcoming major obstacles and opposition in accomplishing something extraordinary that is of service to others. It's not because the successful people of this world get all the breaks; the most successful people play the success game in a completely different way than most people do. They religiously follow The Easy Rule of Life and declare, "Look Ma, life's easy."

Whether you like it or not — and it has been my experience that most people don't — the degree to which you follow The Easy Rule of Life will determine how much satisfaction and happiness you achieve throughout your whole life. Start using The Easy Rule of Life and your life will change remarkably. You will want to kick yourself for having taken so much time to implement it. But at least you will have gotten your life to work at this time, and you can go forward from here.

How long does it take to change your ways and start using The Easy Rule of Life to your advantage? But a second or two. Then the uncomfortable work begins of continuing to utilize The Easy Rule of Life. One day at a time — forever! Repetition makes the master. When you eventually achieve true success in your life by using The Easy Rule of Life, you will joyfully tell yourself, "It's all in how you play the game, isn't it?"

10
Ordinary People Attain Extraordinary Success — You Can Too!

Have you ever thought about someone you know who has succeeded in something quite remarkable? This could be starting a highly successful business, writing a blockbuster-selling book, designing an award-winning house, or going out with a stunning member of the opposite sex. You are wondering how someone like this could pull it off. The individual doesn't appear to have as much talent as you, be as smart as you, or be as attractive as you. If this person can do it, why can't you?

To the extent that you have abilities that come at least as close to those of the average person in society, you are undoubtedly right about the accomplished person not having more talent, intelligence, or sex appeal than you. This shouldn't come as a big surprise. You don't have to be a saint or a genius to make an impact or big difference in this world. Fantasies and dreams don't have to be a waste of time. Truth be known, extraordinary success is attained by ordinary people — who are not much different from you and me.

Practically every spectacular achievement was once thought impossible. What is impossible today to most people may be tomorrow's breakthrough success for some ordinary, but motivated individual. In many cases, one frustrated person is saying, "I give up, it can't be done," while another empowered person is responding to the same situation with "This looks like a great opportunity to create something new and interesting." If you don't think that it can be done, at least get out of the way of the person who is actually doing it.

The difference between success and failure is often pretty slim. It's usually not so much a big difference in people's abilities as a difference in people's self-esteem. Many individuals with great natural ability have been immobilized because of their inability to get their esteem out of the deep ditch in which it rests. If you regularly have bouts of low self-esteem, it is imperative that you do what is necessary to get out of that ditch and raise your concept of yourself. With low self-esteem you will continue to experience frustration and failure. Low self-esteem is a paralyzing disease that invariably produces unhappiness.

Here's the bottom line: Ordinary people attain extraordinary success — you can too! Indeed, you can do something truly spectacular if you refuse to accept that it is impossible. Countless individuals have either worked at lousy jobs, failed miserably at many things, dropped out of school, got rejected hundreds of times, goofed off for years, or did time in jail before achieving extraordinary success.

Within each of us, more than we ever care to admit, lies the power to change our lives. We can have better health, deeper friendships, everlasting love, more riches, enjoyable work, and greater freedom. The power lies not in getting to Heaven, but in using our creativity on Earth.

No matter who you are, you must accept that you have a lot going for you. You must believe in yourself and set reasonable targets for achieving your goals. You may avoid creative and artistic pursuits because you don't think of yourself as creative or artistic. Whether or not you consider yourself artistically inclined, try doing something artistic on a regular basis.

Take at least an hour or two to make a list of your skills, your interests, and your strengths. You will be surprised at how much talent you have. Once you have a firm idea of what you want out of life, you can start working toward attaining it. You must realize the many things that are possible. When you say something can't be done, soon after you will probably see someone doing it. In most cases the person doing it won't have any greater abilities or talent than you.

Set your sights high and you will likely accomplish something truly remarkable in your life. You don't have to be overly ambitious — but you must have enthusiasm and energy. It's a case of making the most of your creativity and will power. Decide what you would like to achieve in life, and then go after it with conviction. In time, other people may be wondering how you could have succeeded in something quite remarkable — even though you aren't as talented, intelligent, attractive, or hardworking as they are!

11

Overnight Success Happens Only in Fairy Tales, Trashy Novels, and Bad Movies

Trying to attain great success in life is like trying to climb a great mountain. They both involve substantial risk, a chance for major disappointment, and a sense of adventure. On your journey to success you will encounter many new problems — but you will encounter many new opportunities and wonderful experiences as well. You must be warned, however, that attaining your goals will likely take a lot longer than you may think. Not only does the mountain always look closer than it is, the mountain gets steeper as you get closer.

Perhaps you have explored your dreams and selected the field in which you would like to succeed. You may want to own a fancy restaurant. You may want to make a big difference in the environmental movement. You may want to make a name for yourself in the field of public speaking. Whatever area you have chosen, be warned that you can't turn ideas into reality overnight. It just isn't going to happen — regardless of how talented, intelligent, or attractive you are.

In North America today, there is a persistent belief that it is possible to make it overnight. One day you are taking singing lessons and the next day you are performing in front of 60,000 screaming fans in New York's Madison Square Garden. One day you are an unknown struggling actor in Peoria, Illinois, and the next day you are turning down roles for some of Hollywood's biggest upcoming movies. One day you are graduating with an MBA and the next day you are running a Fortune 500 company. Magazines, newspapers, radio, television, and the Internet propagate this false belief about the making of overnight sensations.

Fact is, you won't get your name in lights overnight — no matter how much you throw your heart and soul into it. And it probably won't happen in a year or two, or even five. Patience is important. You must take your time in search of fame and fortune, assuming that's what you want to achieve in life.

The great movie director Francis Ford Coppola once claimed, "I've been failing for, like, ten or eleven years. When it turns, it'll turn. Right now I'm just trying to squeeze through a very tight financial period, get the movie out, and put my things in order." As Coppola proved, good things come to people who work at it and are willing to wait.

The important project you start today may bring you fame, fortune, romance, or adventure. It may take five, ten, or even twenty-five years, however. The famous are successful because they finish important and difficult projects. Even in Hollywood, success is in good measure a matter of hanging on after others have let go. "I realized early on that success was tied to not giving up," reflected Harrison Ford. "Most people in this business gave up and went on to other things. If you simply didn't give up, you would outlast the people who came in on the bus with you."

Clearly, success takes staying power and longevity. The fact that success takes so long is a good thing, however. Most people can't handle success, especially if it comes too quickly. That's why American author Elbert Hubbard warned, "Pray that success will not come any faster than you are able to endure it." What's more, if it was possible to attain overnight success, no one would get real satisfaction from it.

Trust me on this one: Overnight success happens only in fairy tales, trashy novels, and bad movies. Given what is involved in achieving success, you will attain success much faster when you take your time and aren't desperate for it. If you want to be a success in any particular field, whether it's in movies or computers, it pays to stick around for awhile.

Shoot for conquering the world of business or politics by the year 2017 or 2027 — instead of 2010. This way your chances will be increased dramatically. Above all, be patient because anything worth having takes time.

12
To Know and Not to Do Is Not
Yet to Know

Think you know a lot? Think again. It is commonly accepted in Western society that knowledge is power. Not necessarily so! Knowledge is power only if you use it — and use it properly. Put another way, don't tell the world about how much you know if you aren't going to use your knowledge for anything but talk.

The Buddhists have a proverb: "To know and not to do is not yet to know." Needless to say, knowledge and wisdom are useless if you don't use them to accomplish something worthwhile. If you are to make an important difference in this world, you must put your blue-chip knowledge in synch with your deepest values and beliefs and pursue what you truly want out of life.

Fact is, action speaks louder than words — even a little bit of action is worth much more than a whole lot of talking. Remember the old expression, "Talk is cheap because supply always exceeds demand." Great ideas and knowledge are the stuff from which great success is made. Nonetheless, great ideas and knowledge by themselves won't make a person successful.

You can learn a lot by watching others, but there comes a time when you have to do something for your own satisfaction. Sitting back and watching the world go by is no way to achieve satisfaction. On the contrary, it's a highly effective way to achieve dissatisfaction — and who needs dissatisfaction?

You must walk the talk if you are to make your mark on the world. "All know the way," observed sixth-century Indian Buddhist monk Bodhidharma. "Few actually walk it." Clearly, words have to be put into action. You will be disgusted with yourself if you keep talking about it, but never quite get around to doing it. Your ideas can change the world, but only when accompanied with action.

I believe that it was British mathematician and philosopher Alfred North Whitehead who once said that ideas won't keep — that something must be done about them. An acquaintance of mine has a million ideas and seems happiest when he's expounding on one of them. He never gets around to trying out any, however, because he is always generating more. The lesson here is that the successful implementation of one good idea is worth more than a million ideas not acted upon.

Your great idea will never see the light of day if you aren't motivated enough to follow through with your insights and aspirations. Intuition, creativity, and will power are your greatest assets. Your "great" idea is just an idea. And that's where it will remain — an idea — if you just talk about it. The idea will become a great one when you make something out of it.

You have to spend less time thinking and more time doing. The thing that separates successful people from the less successful ones is that the successful people are always taking part in interesting journeys. They are doers. The less successful are not doers. They may be interested in destinations, but resist making the necessary journeys. Without journeys come no new destinations.

This applies to the best-selling book that you are capable of writing — or any other project that you are capable of completing, but haven't got around to doing. Begin today and see where it takes you. "The distance doesn't matter," French literary patron Madame Marquise du Deffand pointed out. "Only the first step is difficult."

Suffice it to say that you only truly know something valuable if you live it. Now is the time to undertake that project that may change your life. Make it different, make it challenging, and make it radical. Above all, make sure you undertake it. Do it badly — but at least do it! The world needs more people who get things done — instead of just talking about how to get things done.

13

Always Expect the Unexpected Because the Only Certainty Is Uncertainty

As much as we can do to improve our lives, we do have to remember that there is no such thing as a sure thing. Rich or poor, every person's future is uncertain. Tomorrow will bring both pain and pleasure. You will have little or no control over many things that happen in the future. All told, the success of the important project is not guaranteed — regardless of how much talent you have and how much effort you put into it.

One reason is that Murphy's Law has a habit of throwing a wrench into the best of plans. In case you haven't been introduced to Murphy's Law, allow me to do so. Murphy's Law says, "Nothing is as easy as it looks. Everything takes longer than you expect. And if anything can go wrong — it will at the worst possible moment."

Although Murphy's Law is far too pessimistic, it's worth remembering nonetheless. Not all things go wrong at the worst possible moment, but many do. Indeed, sometimes even if something cannot go wrong — it still will!

As a matter of course there will always be unexpected disruptions in our lives. Notice that when you remodel your house, things usually take twice as long to complete and cost twice as much as expected. Career, travel, marriage, and leisure plans are all subject to unexpected negative influences. You may be riding high one day, but all good things do come to an end. Don't expect your feeling of being in control of the world to last forever. Trust me, it won't.

Things will change. What is uncertain is when things will change. Unexpected events can throw you off stride for a minute, a day, or even a few years. Keep in mind that it's the big changes in life that rarely give any advance warning. Obstacles in your path can appear out of nowhere. Anything worth doing is likely to take longer than you expect. Things for which we have high expectations sometimes have to be abandoned entirely. If it's important to you, it's wise to be prepared for something unexpected.

What is most certain is uncertainty. The future will bring change. It is important to learn how to adapt to rapidly changing circumstances because in this day and age there will be many. We can resist change, but it's going to happen anyway. Perhaps it's the short-term pain that comes with a lot of change that we fear and resist.

Those who are flexible in their thinking and their ways will prosper despite forthcoming upheavals in the way we live and do things. Not surprisingly, studies show that individuals who respond creatively to change live longer than those who don't. Even in the bleakest situations, these people find a ray of sunshine. They know that change can be uncomfortable, but often it leads to something much better in the long run.

Be prepared to change with the times — instead of resisting change — and you will be happier and more relaxed. The silver lining of the uncertainty principle is that life's most treasured moments often come unannounced. Rather than being threatened by unexpected developments, we should learn that they can also be hidden opportunities. Disasters hit our plans, but so does unanticipated good luck.

Being concerned about the future is pointless. The future will be here sooner than you can imagine. It's crazy, but the harder it becomes to predict life's events, the more we try to rely on predictions. There are no statistics on the future — aside from the fact that it is always ahead of you and it will come one day at a time. The best policy is to expect the unexpected. The only thing for certain is that nothing is for certain. Trust your instincts and creativity to help you on life's journey and you will do just fine.

14

Too Much Safety Is Dangerous
for Your Well-Being

"No one from the beginning of time has had security," proclaimed American diplomat and writer Eleanor Roosevelt. Her words are ones to ponder carefully. Security is one of those things most — if not all — people strive for all of their lives. The dark side of security, however, is that it is an illusion at best. Too much safety, in fact, is dangerous for your well-being. In more cases than you can ever imagine, the bigger risk is in not taking the risk.

As a matter of course we all have a tendency to grow comfortable with existing conditions — even those that do us absolutely no good (there are many forms of mental illness). For instance, in the workplace we end up tolerating dead-end jobs, professions we dislike, and companies that mistreat us. Of course, we resist making changes because we fear the unknown.

You yourself may have settled into a comfortable and predictable routine. There comes a time, however, when you have to find something that will stretch your talents more. You must have faith in yourself. When your instincts tempt you to take a risk on something that is not a life-and-death matter, then do so with confidence.

If you are dissatisfied with your career choice, the greatest risk may be in not leaving your job. Don't wait for the right time to quit. It's best to do it now because there is never a right time. There is risk involved in most important decisions. A recent survey by the Royal Bank of Canada showed that successful entrepreneurs, who left their secure jobs to be on their own, believed taking chances made them stronger and wiser. Paradoxically, by taking the road with more risks, they achieved more security.

Of course, risk-taking can be dangerous for sensation-seekers. So don't be rash and risk losing everything you have. It's not intelligent to take extremely high or uncertain risks. Wise people take calculated risks. The key is to take smart risks instead of stupid ones. If you are a fifty-year-old man, you stand a one-in-two-hundred chance of dying in the next year. Since you may not be around in any event, why not take some calculated risks that may pay back big dividends in happiness and satisfaction?

Contrary to popular wisdom, the risk of taking action can be less than the risk of inaction. Life is a perilous journey at best. Incredible romance, remarkable fame, and outstanding success are attained by those individuals who take substantial risks. On one hand, you can play it totally safe and wind up with what you already have to your name — you may even wind up with less. On the other hand, you can take a few risks and cash in on a few wonderful opportunities and wind up with a lot more of the things you would like out of life.

Traveling on a risk-free road, unfortunately, won't get you to any important destination. Unfavorable odds shouldn't keep you from pursuing what you know intuitively you were meant to do. Many people will criticize you for attempting those things that they wouldn't dare attempt themselves. Cowards, who would like you to remain a coward, should be ignored. There is a time you have to be courageous and dive into the unknown with the intention of swimming with what fate brings your way. Happiness and satisfaction will be much more forthcoming when you have the courage to pursue your convictions.

When your inner voice is telling you to take a risk, it's best to do so even though your rational mind may be telling you otherwise. Following the tried and proven path may appear the safest. In some ways it is. But blazing your own trail will bring you more adventure and satisfaction and leave tracks for others to see. Conversely, you won't leave any tracks following a trail that's heavily traveled by the masses.

If the path you have taken in life feels really safe, then likely it is not the right path. When you look back on your life, you'll regret the things you didn't attempt more than the ones you did and at which you failed. The virtue of risk-taking is emphasized in this old adage: "Someone who tries to do something and fails is a lot better off than the person who tries to do nothing and succeeds."

15
You Can Observe a Lot Just by Watching

A successful American entrepreneur had acquired a lot of wealth. He decided to retire and take it easy, living a life to which most people aspire. Unfortunately, he soon realized that he still wasn't happy. Because his life was so empty, the entrepreneur decided to go in search of a Zen master who apparently knew three important secrets for living life to the fullest.

After many months of searching, the entrepreneur finally found the Zen master on top of an obscure mountain. The Zen master was happy to reveal the three secrets to having a happy and satisfying life. The entrepreneur was surprised by what he was told. According to the Zen master, the three secrets to having a happy and fulfilling life are:

- Pay attention
- Pay attention
- Pay attention

Indeed, we all should pay more attention than we do. Most of us walk around the majority of the time as if we were sleeping, paying little regard to what is going on around us. Some philosophers say most of us are unconscious most of the time. Author Peter Leschak commented on the unconsciousness of human beings, "All of us are watchers — of television, of time clocks, of traffic on the freeway — but few are observers. Everyone is looking; not many are seeing."

Few of us see the best solutions to our life's problems that are often staring us in the face. Even the obvious escapes us. A character in Joseph Heller's *Catch 22* had flies in his eyes. He couldn't see these flies in his eyes, however. Reason: The flies in his eyes prevented him from seeing these same flies in his eyes. We are like this character. "The obscure we see eventually," remarked American broadcast journalist Edward R. Murrow. "The completely obvious, it seems, takes longer."

Those of us who pay little or no attention are the ones who wind up at the bus depot — instead of the harbor where we should be — when our ships finally come in. According to French poet Paul Valéry, "The best way to make your dreams come true is to wake up." Particularly important is paying attention to those things that matter. It's easy to be caught by surprise when you are focusing on something that doesn't matter. Failure to pay attention to the things that matter will result in your being blind-sighted by some destructive event that you should have seen coming.

If you are aware of how vision works, you know that what you see initially is just a fraction of what actually exists. Take a stroll down a street that you have walked on many times before. Take your time to carefully observe everything you can. You will be amazed at the many interesting things you have never noticed before. How right legendary American baseball player Yogi Berra was when he remarked, "You can observe a lot just by watching."

Paying attention to the world around you — looking at commonplace things and seeing the miraculous — will lead you to opportunities that others don't see. Opportunities for creating new sources of income, for instance, are all around us, including our backyards. Robert G. Allen and Mark Victor Hansen, co-authors of *The One Minute Millionaire*, claim that they will be able to spot at least fifteen moneymaking opportunities in your living room alone. Pay attention to the world around you and there should be no lack of opportunities available to you. If anything, there will likely be too many.

Expanding your awareness involves bringing a fresh perspective to familiar experiences. One of the keys to enjoying the world more is to practice the habit of flexibility. As an old Dutch proverb points out, "In the land of the blind, one eye is king." Pay attention and you will see a whole of things in this world that others don't see.

You must come to terms with the fact that perception is everything. What you see is what you get. Stop functioning on automatic pilot. Be attentive and you will see a myriad of interesting and exciting things happening in the world around you. Change your vision and you can change your life.

16
Don't Mess Around with Reality and Reality Won't Mess Around with You

According to a Zen proverb, "If you understand, things are just as they are; if you do not understand, things are just as they are." Reality, in other words, is the way it is, regardless of how much or how little we understand about life. One of the biggest barriers that will hold us back in this world is the big difference between what life is and what we think life ought to be.

To be sure, false expectations about the world can be paralyzing to our human psyche. The majority of people spend way too much time idealizing how things ought to be — and way too little time observing and accepting how things really are. They develop a theoretical understanding of the way this world ought to be, and then try living life as if this were true.

Unfortunately, fantasies about how the world ought to be tend to obscure how the world really is. People lose sight of reality and then wonder why they can't make things work out the way they would like. At the extreme, they end up being swept along by negative events without an understanding of what really is going on.

As a matter of course reality sets certain rules for playing the game of life. It is essential that we learn these rules. Only a muddlehead persists in playing a game without learning the rules. Reality can be harsh, but you better respect it. Mess around with reality and it will knock you down every time. Conversely, if you don't mess around with reality, then it won't mess around with you.

Reality doesn't care how good your intentions are. If you mess around with gravity — and reality — by walking off the roof of a ten-story building, you will pay dearly for it. This may earn you the no-brainer-of-the-week award — but not much more. Reality won't care that you were testing a new product to help humanity. The fact that you were a decent person with good intentions won't make a bit of difference.

After all, life doesn't care how we would like it to be. Sure, the rich ought to make less money and the poor ought to make more. There ought to be better public-funded healthcare for everyone. The government should build better freeways so our commuting time is cut to twenty minutes from an hour and a half. Wow! This is starting to sound awesome indeed! It's easy to let our imaginations run wild about how things ought to be. Fact is, nonetheless, it won't make any difference how much time we put into thinking about how life should be. Life will remain the way it is.

An inscription in an Amsterdam cathedral reads, "It is so. It cannot be otherwise." This doesn't mean that you shouldn't think about changing something distasteful in this world. Think about changing it and then work toward it. While attempting to change something, you must still deal with reality. Unexpected events will derail your plans. It may take countless years of blood, sweat, and tears before you see any results. You may not even see any results. It ought to be easier, but it won't be.

As harsh as reality is at times, facing reality can be good for you. A big and hard dose of reality can do wonders for your life. You can change your life dramatically the day you start living according to the way things are instead of the way they should be. Keep in mind that with the right attitude and substantial effort, reality can be much more interesting and rewarding than fantasy.

Putting things in the best possible way, life will never be the way we want it to be or the way it ought to be. Accepting reality for what it is will liberate you from the imprisonment of what ought to be. Most of our disappointments are due to our belief that life should be different from what it actually is. You are unlikely to be happy and satisfied in this world unless you see life as what it truly is — and not some fantasy representing what you would like it to be.

"What is, is," proclaimed Lenny Bruce, "and what ought to be is a damn lie." The bigger the difference between what is and what we think that life ought to be — the bigger the lie we are likely to live. Get it out of your head that life should be a bowl of cherries. If you don't, you will only succeed in mastering the arts of nervous twitching and driving yourself insane.

17

If You Don't Want to Accomplish Something Important, Any Excuse Will Do

It is unfortunate that so many people in our society accept blaming others and making excuses as valid tools to explain their shortcomings and predicaments in their lives. In fact, people fall in love with their excuses for why they are stuck in their present positions and why they are getting nowhere in life.

Although many people actually believe their own excuses, these individuals don't realize that most excuses serve absolutely no valuable purpose. Excuses are lies, false statements deliberately presented as being true, meant to deceive others and the excuse-makers themselves. Excuses are used to cover up such things as laziness, low self-esteem, and the fear of failure.

To be sure, excuses are easy to fabricate. These are some of the favorites that others use: If I weren't married with children; if I had a higher education; if I had nicer parents; if the economy were better; if I had more breaks in life; if I weren't so far in debt; and if my nose weren't so long.

Perhaps you need some new excuses — besides the ones you already have — to convince yourself that you can't improve your life for the better. Luckily for you, I can help. I used to be an expert at making excuses and even earned my Master's in Excuse-Making before I gave up excuses so that I could have a better life. Here are a few gems that even David Letterman would like:

Top Ten Excuses Not to Improve Your Life

1. I don't believe people can have a really good life unless they are offspring of Edison or Einstein.
2. I once had a nosebleed and I am afraid of getting more if I put more effort into improving my life.
3. George W. Bush would think I was unpatriotic if I gave up my lousy job in corporate America and pursued my dream job.
4. Finding a dream job that I love may be too relaxing — I think I feel more comfortable tense.
5. I am three-times divorced and my conservative estimate is that I have at least twelve kids.

6. I prefer to live in the past because most of my life has been spent there.
7. I have arthritis, and although I know people with much more serious disabilities have been extraordinarily successful in their lives, I don't think they know what it is like to have arthritis.
8. Although my life is boring and sad, I kind of like it — I may actually be addicted to boredom and sadness.
9. My dog died and I need to get another one real fast.
10. I am afraid of becoming a member of a better class of people.

No doubt these should be more than enough. You may find some of the above excuses handy for explaining all your shortcomings in life — particularly when you don't want to take responsibility for having created these shortcomings. My point is best made by a Jewish proverb: "If you don't want to do something, one excuse is as good as another."

Let's be honest. All of us are good at justifying why we haven't been more successful in life. I have likely done it at least 10,000 times myself and still fall into the trap at one time or another. Alas, no one is ever remotely happy with the results attained from excuses; we hurt only ourselves with excuses.

If you create a great excuse why you aren't able to accomplish something important in your life, you will be shipwrecked even before you get aboard. Fact is, virtually all excuse-makers progress at the same speed just like all procrastinators wait at the same speed. Moreover, there is no time like the present to use an excuse to postpone what is difficult, but important.

But you must not postpone what is important. For instance, if you are no longer inspired by your job, if you are not learning something new and exciting every day, you must escape your job before you become brain dead. No excuses! Mark Twain once pointed out that "There are 1,000 excuses for every failure but never a good reason."

Excuses are convenient, but as always, there is a dark side to anything convenient. Individuals who are not able to get rid of excuses find it virtually impossible to succeed in the long term. On the flip side, people who don't use excuses succeed at a lot more things than they think they can — and end up making a tremendous difference in this world.

18
Self-Pity Costs Nothing and It Is Worth Just As Much

A great mystery to the successful of this world is why so many people choose to be victims — instead of empowering themselves to do something positive with their lives. In this day and age being a victim is even trendy. For instance, the media are always looking for victims to feature in their stories. In a society that actually promotes the victim mentality as acceptable — and in some cases, desirable — it takes a strong personality to be motivated and empowered enough to resist being a victim and instead make a positive difference in this world.

Of course, there are many true victims in this world. People who have been victimized by criminals, drunk drivers, and oppressive third-world governments have the right to complain about their predicaments and demand justice. Nonetheless, at the risk of appearing callous, I have to say that even someone who has been genuinely victimized shouldn't continue to be a victim. After a certain point, there is no payoff. Humorist Josh Billings quipped, "Pity costs nothing, and it ain't worth nothing."

For many individuals it's all too easy and irresistible to assume the victim mentality. They look at themselves as victims when, if fact, they aren't. These individuals look at this world as a rip-off due to their position in life. Blame for their unhappiness and loneliness is directed at society, their parents, their country's economic state, or the world in general. The thing that is impressive about people with the victim mentality is how much energy they will put into shunning responsibility and complicating their lives.

Unfortunately, self-proclaimed victims seldom accomplish anything worthwhile — to say nothing of the disappointment and grief they put themselves through. Being a victim may make you feel secure and comfortable because it's familiar territory. There are no real payoffs, however.

If you are dealing with a troubled past and facing an uncertain future, victimhood is no way to get your life in order. You must face the consequences.

People with the victim mentality spend months, or even years, passing blame, and never get around to taking responsibility for actually solving their problems. They never experience happiness as long as they continue to see themselves as helpless victims of fate. As soon as they start enjoying life, they find reasons not to enjoy it. Their identity of victim has to be preserved at all costs — even happiness. The role of victim looking to be victimized becomes their sole driving force in life.

In her book *Fire Your Shrink*, Michele Wiener-Davis, a well-known professional therapist, focuses on the dangers of the victim mentality. She explains why therapy usually doesn't work for most people who see "shrinks." Wiener-Davis cites individuals who used to suffer from the victim mentality, but now have become winners by turning their lives around. She claims: "People who live their dreams are those who stop considering all the angles, weighing the pros and cons, and just do it. They've come to realize it's time to stop talking to their friends, families, or therapists, and begin living. Without action there is no change."

When you are feeling sorry for yourself, remember that self-pity costs nothing and it's worth just as much. Regardless of how much circumstances influence your life, you can always control how you react to them. Taking responsibility for your thoughts and actions will liberate you from the need to pass blame onto others, society, or the government.

The real rewards in life come from having made a significant difference in this world. No doubt this is much easier said than done. In many respects, however, you are probably limiting yourself in what you can accomplish in your lifetime. In short, it's not what life hands you — it's how you respond to it that counts. The more you look for opportunity in adversity, the more you will find it. Start capitalizing on all the opportunities that confront you and you won't have time to be a victim.

19

You Can Be a Victim or You Can Be Successful —
You Can't Be Both, However

Sadly, it's all too easy and irresistible for most humans to play the victim game. The thing that is impressive about self-proclaimed victims is how tenacious they are in directing their energy into shunning responsibility and complicating their lives.

I hope that you won't fall into the trap of experiencing victimhood too often — given that people who do so are seldom successful. Claiming you are a victim is the ultimate expression of selfishness because you are basically saying that "everything is about me." If you play the victim game, you should get yourself one of those T-shirts that says, "Yes, it is all about me."

The truth is, it's not all about you. It never has been and it never will be. With one trivial exception, this world is made of 6.5 billion other human beings, a good portion of them with minds thinking in one form or another, "It's all about me." If it's all about you, then do something — everything possible — for yourself. Don't expect any of the 6.5 billion others to do something for you. You will be waiting a long, long time.

Victims are known for their incredible ability to complain, which is probably the worst possible thing you can do if you want to succeed at anything. Complaining keeps you a sufferer and does nothing to liberate you. When you are constantly a victim, you remain in a rut — and the only major difference between a rut and a grave is the dimensions!

If you want to get out of the rut, you must stop being the victim. Clearly, if you have been passing blame for your shortcomings, now is the time to stop — not tomorrow, but today. Stop blaming society. Stop blaming the education system. Stop blaming the government. Stop blaming the President. Stop blaming the economy.

So the mystery deepens. Who or what else is left to blame? Yourself, of course! Who is responsible for your life situation? "If your daily life seems poor, do not blame it; blame yourself," German poet and novelist Rainer Maria

Rilke reminded us. "Tell yourself that you are not poet enough to call forth its riches."

Blaming yourself in a positive way is the best way to respond to your shortcomings and setbacks. After you have signed an agreement or contract of sorts, for instance, it's pointless to blame anyone else when you discover the terms aren't as generous to you as you had initially thought. Having failed to read the small print is your fault and no one else's. You have no option but to fulfill your part of the contract. You may not have gotten as much as you had anticipated — but you did get an important extra you hadn't anticipated. The bonus is the lesson that from now on you should read the small print carefully.

The day you start blaming yourself in a positive way is the day you are well on your way to a life that works. Winners blame themselves; losers blame others. Are you overextended financially like most people in Western society today? If you want to be in a better financial position than the masses, blame yourself; you are a victim of your own scheming. It's time to take control of your life and find ways to either reduce your spending or earn more money.

The choice is yours. Either you can be a victim or you can be successful — you can't be both, however. With the self-imposed suffering that invariably accompanies a victim mentality, you are three-quarters of the way to defeat without even having started. Blaming others will keep you on the road to perpetual failure.

Still don't believe this? Well, I have yet to go to an awards celebration where the person with the most blame of others and personal excuses for not accomplishing anything significant was featured as the main attraction.

20
If Something Is Boring You,
It's Probably You

"Is not life a hundred times too short for us to bore ourselves?" asked Friedrich Nietzsche. The obvious answer is: "Yes!" Boredom, even so, is a condition that affects millions of North Americans. Boredom deprives people of the meaning of life and undermines their zest for living. Although it would seem to specifically affect those who are idle and jobless, people with high-status and well-paying careers can be just as affected.

To a certain degree we all get bored some time in our lives. Ironically, many of the things we strive for can end up boring us; a new job, in time, becomes boring. An exciting relationship can become dull. Leisure activities once deemed precious may feel like wasted time. After a few years, living in vibrant New York may end up feeling dull and uninteresting.

The key to conquering boredom is taking full responsibility for having caused it. Particularly if you have wasted the first part of your adult life on boring work, you certainly don't want to be like so many individuals who waste the second part of their adult lives on a boring retirement. "In order to live free and happily," Richard Bach warned us, "you must sacrifice boredom. It is not always an easy sacrifice."

People who cherish and can handle freedom undoubtedly are seldom bored. Their capacity to grow and their ability to choose are indispensable for handling the free time that a balanced lifestyle affords. Unfortunately, not all individuals — even well-educated and highly intelligent ones — are able to handle freedom and avoid boredom.

How well-educated and highly intelligent individuals can excel in the workplace and yet fail so miserably at leisure is one of the sadder aspects of human existence. On the other hand, how millions of individuals covering the full spectrum of education, intelligence, and income levels can be just as happy involved in leisure pursuits as they can in the workplace is one of the positive aspects of human existence.

Given that life offers us so much in the way of interesting pursuits, to be bored is to retire from life. You want your leisure life to be more than just something to do when you aren't working or sleeping. Whether you avoid boredom and depression will be determined by the nature of your leisure activities. You must not commit the grave mistake of making the couch, the fridge, and the TV your three best friends. This trio not only contributes to boredom big time; it also contributes to poor mental and physical health.

The word "boredom" should not even be part of your vocabulary. As French novelist Jules Renard commented, "Being bored is an insult to oneself." You as a creative individual have the ability to pursue interesting activities. Creative expression is the natural inclination of life. Keep reminding yourself that life can be a series of adventures and wonderful discoveries because deep down you are a creative person and not a boring one.

The next time you are so bored that you would get excited about an invitation to the opening of a new garbage dump, remind yourself who is responsible for your boredom. To conquer boredom, you must get to the source. Be clear that there is only one source. If you still don't get it, perhaps these wise words of Welsh poet Dylan Thomas may be of some help: "Somebody is boring me . . . I think it's me."

Yes, indeed! If something is boring you, it's probably you. Handling boredom is actually quite easy. Get busy doing the things you love, or something that you have always wanted to do. Your taking absolute responsibility for your boredom is the creative force that will make it go away.

21
All Worry Is Wasted

Worrying about the trivial — and occasionally the important — is one of the more popular activities in North America today. Worry is so rampant that many people spend several hours a day in this dubious activity. A substantial number of Americans — 15 percent, in fact — spend at least 50 percent of each day worrying about their lives, says a study from Pennsylvania State University.

On this note, you should give serious consideration to the number of hours that you spend worrying each day. One hour a day means that you are spending 365 hours a year having worrisome thoughts. Yet spending only one hour a week in this activity is probably too much. You may have already realized that most worry is self-inflicted and a great deal of it is useless.

At best, worrying is an activity that robs you of precious time. Excessive worry can have much more serious consequences, however. Some researchers claim approximately one out of three people in North America ends up with serious mental problems as a result of worry. Worry predisposes people to stress, headaches, panic attacks, ulcers, and other related ailments.

Sadly, we all spend way too much time worrying about matters that don't matter at all. For instance, you have likely noticed that if you take off those "Do Not Remove" tags from pillows and mattresses, nothing bad — in fact, nothing at all — happens to you.

Studies show that 40 percent of our worries are about events that will never happen, 30 percent of our worries are about events that already happened or have progressed too far for us to change, 22 percent of our worries are about trivial events, 4 percent of our worries are about real events we cannot change, and only 4 percent of our worries are about real events on which we can act.

This means that 96 percent of our worrying is wasted because it is directed at things we can't control. In fact, since we can control the remaining 4 percent of events we worry about, this worrying is also wasted effort. The bottom line is that 100 percent of our efforts put into worrying is to no avail. This is why Mitzi Chandler concluded, "Worry is as useless as a handle on a snowball."

One way to deal with worry is to challenge the thoughts that are the basis of your worry. What are the chances that the feared event will even happen? What are the worst- and the best-case scenarios if the event happens? What are the chances of the worst-case scenarios and the best-case scenarios happening? Have you ever successfully handled similar events with no serious effects on your life?

Another effective way to handle worry is to get immersed in positive events that distract you from your worrisome thoughts. Getting immersed in something positive is an incredible force in shifting the mind away from the worries of the day. Fill your life with hope, dreams, and creative pursuits instead of worry.

Needless to say, if all worry is wasted, it can't have any significant positive effects on our lives. Coming up with creative ideas for earning money or attaining real success is difficult when you are worrying most of the time. Moreover, even if you do manage to generate a creative idea or two, ideas produced in such a state will prove to be useless. Undoubtedly, if you worry a lot, you will be too afraid to take risks in implementing ideas, regardless of how remarkable they may be.

In short, most people think that worrying serves some worthwhile purpose when, in fact, the opposite is true. The final score on worry is that all of it is wasted. At the extreme, worrying makes problems worse in the long term. Clearly, fear and worry won't help you solve problems and achieve your goals in a relaxed manner. Instead, these emotions will drain you of energy and keep you from attaining the desirable things in life that you are capable of attaining.

Excessive worry not only hinders creativity; it stifles our goals, hopes, desires, dreams, and prosperity. Worrying about problems is like looking at your nasty neighbors through high-power binoculars. The problems don't disappear; they end up appearing a lot larger — and much nastier — than they really are.

22
Procrastination Is the Art of Keeping Up with Yesterday

Nothing comes quite so easily to us as the ability to procrastinate. With varying degrees, we all have the tendency to let things slide. In fact, most of us could write the Bible on time-wasting — but there again, we would never get around to putting this project together regardless of how much promise it offered. We always have too many much more important activities to pursue — such as sleeping, watching television, surfing the Internet for twisted humor, and checking out absolutely useless e-mails.

It's okay to put off the projects and tasks that have little significance to us. The problem is that some of us keep putting off the most critical of our projects, and keep spending time on those that don't really matter. A reading from the Hebrew prayer book Mahzor states: "We often wait too long to do what must be done today, in a world that gives us only one day at a time, without any assurance of tomorrow."

The key to getting your life in order is to meet your own expectations of yourself in starting and completing worthwhile projects. Putting off crucial chores, errands, and quests is not only harmful to your self-esteem; it is harmful to your health. According to researchers, since procrastination creates stress — and stress is harmful to health — hard-core procrastinators have higher rates of headaches, gastric problems, backaches, colds, and infections. Because everyone procrastinates, researchers define hard-core procrastinators as those who put off something in every aspect of their lives.

Putting things in the best possible way, a graffiti writer announced, "Procrastination is the art of keeping up with yesterday." You may be tempted to ignore a big problem hoping it will go away. It's okay to ignore trivial matters, and let them take care of themselves, but you can't escape the big problems by pretending they don't exist. Unfortunately, the big problems, if not addressed, have a habit of getting even bigger instead of going away on their own accord. Even certain small tasks will become big tasks if you put them off long enough.

More often than not it's a good idea to confront a problem as soon as possible and get it over with. Dealing with the problem can be unpleasant and stressful in the short term, but if handled properly, the long-term benefits will last a lifetime and change your life dramatically in the process. Keep in mind that if you don't take action, the problem will remain in your life indefinitely.

Putting off your crucial projects today means that their status will be the same tomorrow as it was yesterday. There will be times when you realize what has to be done, but, for some mysterious reason, you keep putting it off. You must do whatever it takes to get yourself started. If the project is important to you, sooner or later you must act. Taking the first step is the hardest — often this is half of the battle.

Comedian Stephen Wright claimed, "I am writing a book. I have the pages numbered so far." Another area where procrastination rears its ugly head is in projects started, but only partially completed. Starting the project may be half the battle, but you must keep the momentum going. If the project at hand has any significance at all, it is best to complete it before new ones are undertaken.

It's a reasonable assumption that your goal is to get to tomorrow, and not just keep up with yesterday. Then today is the time to make plans for those paramount projects, instead of just thinking about them. Having decided that something is worthwhile, you must start today regardless of your excuses. Today, not tomorrow, is the day you should start writing the book that you want to write. Today, not tomorrow, is the day you should start exercising to enhance your fitness and health. And today, not tomorrow, is the day you should spend time with the children instead of working overtime.

Conquering procrastination takes planning, effort, will power, and self-confidence. Those who believe they can, will — and those who don't believe they can, won't. The good news, according to researchers, is we procrastinate less as we age, at which time we learn how not to procrastinate. Undertaking those major projects will put you in charge of your life and place you on the road to better and bigger things. You will be well on your way to happily welcoming tomorrow — instead of unhappily keeping up with yesterday.

23

Don't Buy Expensive Socks If You Can Never Find Them

Do you want a full, relaxed, satisfying, and happy life? Begin by making organization one of your strongest assets. Perhaps you realized a long time ago how favorably your life functions when you are well-organized and how things get out of hand when you are terribly disorganized. Indeed, being well-organized puts you in control of your life.

Fact is, we are not born organized; organization is a learned skill that anyone can master. Organized people get the very best out of life because they get the important projects completed and are constantly achieving their goals. They are seldom wasting time being distracted by frivolous activities, searching for lost items, or redoing time-consuming projects. Best of all, they find the time they need to do the things they love and to spend time with the people they care about.

Organization is the art of using your time and resources efficiently. If you would like to get everything done when it's due — without frustration, guilt, or stress — you need to master the art of being orderly. Plain and simple, organization involves planning. Inadequate or no planning goes hand in hand with a chaotic lifestyle. Paradoxically, if you are well-organized, you can afford to be spontaneous and do something that you hadn't planned for the day.

To keep your life functioning harmoniously, keep things simple. This applies as much to your personal life as it does to your work life. Don't buy expensive socks if you can never find them. You don't want to spend precious time looking for your expensive socks in the morning while your co-workers and competitors are already in the office. When you let things get out of hand in one area of your life, other areas of your life will be affected as well. A terribly disorganized personal life will spill over into your work life. Likewise, a chaotic work life will disrupt your personal life.

There may be areas in your personal life on which you have to spend more time so that your work life functions better. Being well-organized means that you are using an efficient system that allows you to locate everything you need when you need it. When your non-career activities — such as friendships, marital matters, family affairs, and house chores — are in turmoil, you will be limited in what you can accomplish in your business or career.

Being truly productive at work gives you more time for activities in your personal life. An orderly life also helps you enjoy your leisure time more, since you don't have to feel guilty about not having accomplished as much at work as you would have liked. What's more, you will feel better at the end of the day when you have time to relax and fit in something that you hadn't planned.

To be better organized at work, set priorities and focus your energy where it will make the most difference. Focus on the most lucrative activities and cut back on the least productive ones. Another key to being well-organized is being able to avoid distractions. It's all too easy to forget what's important. There is no end to distractions — co-workers wanting to gossip, nebulous reports to read, football games to watch on TV, friends demanding attention, etc. — that can interfere with getting critical matters handled quickly.

Contrary to what many people believe, disorganization takes more time than organization. What's more, disorganization ensures that huge obstacles are always directly in the path of getting critical projects completed. Organization is the art of scheduling every day with enough useful activities to make it productive. Never overload your day, however. Your daily schedule should always allow — no exceptions — for leisure activities and enough flexibility to be spontaneous.

If your life is presently in disarray, the time to start being better organized is not tomorrow — the right time is today. When you become well-organized, others will be asking how you are able to make things seem so easy. You will have them wondering how you find the time to complete the essential activities, and still have time to be lazy and leisurely. Make organization your forte and you will have the full, relaxed, satisfying, and happy life to which millions of individuals only aspire.

24
Book Smart Does Not
Mean Life Smart

No doubt you have noticed that many people with a Ph.D. degree aren't very happy — and some of the happiest people in this world don't even know what a Ph.D. is! Contrary to popular belief, education has little to do with how much happiness and satisfaction people get out of life. What's more, an individual can have a fancy education, but still not be very wise. In other words, book smart does not mean life smart.

Upon graduation, many university students believe that they are the elite of humanity, destined to experience incredible fame, fortune, adventure, and romance at an early age. After several years in the work force, however, they may be trapped working on meaningless projects, without any hope of creative fulfillment, joy, and personal success. Even the most brilliant of university graduates may wind up going nowhere emotionally, financially, or socially.

Here's the bottom line: There is a big difference between intellectual people and intelligent people. Ironically, many intellectuals have a hard time distinguishing between the two. Thus, the words by an unknown wise person: "Education is what helps a lot of folks get along without intelligence."

Seymour Epstein, a researcher and psychologist at the University of Massachusetts, agrees. He found that emotional intelligence is more powerful than academic intelligence. Epstein's research indicates that emotional intelligence — being life smart — is crucial for life success.

Emotional intelligence has little to do with our IQ or education. Emotional intelligence involves taking action about a situation rather than complaining about it. It also entails the ability not to take things personally and not to fret about what others think. Being life smart determines a great range of life's successes, from salaries and promotions, to satisfying human relations, to physical and emotional health.

Study the behaviors and attitudes of the truly successful of this world and you will discover that being intellectual is not what makes them peak performers. A recent survey found that high school was the highest level of education for 30 percent of wealthy entrepreneurs. To be sure, the successful people of this world did not learn the secrets of handling failure and inner mobility at universities or colleges. They learned these secrets in the arena called life by doing and not just thinking about doing.

Clearly, many underlying factors help determine an individual's mental, physical, and spiritual health. It may come as a surprise to some people that a degree from Harvard or Stanford is not essential for being life smart. A university degree doesn't teach people how to deal with the pressures of life or how to attain happiness and satisfaction. A university student may learn what is wrong with the economy but not how to make a comfortable living as an entrepreneur in a depressed economy.

"We receive three educations," according to the French philosopher Charles de Montesquieu: "One from our parents, one from our schoolmasters, and one from the world. The third contradicts all that the first two teach us." The really important things you learn in life are the result of your real education — an education that has nothing to do with the curricula in place at schools and universities. You acquire this education through your personal experiences, far removed from your formal education.

You probably know several people who have less formal education than you do but who have attained remarkable success in some field. You may also know others who have a limited education and make a great living. These people should be sufficient evidence that you are capable of the same. You do not need more formal education; what you need is to be more life smart.

Being life smart is having the ability to assess situations and then take action accordingly. A doctorate can't take the place of real-life experiences combined with the powers of imagination, motivation, and action. If you are thinking of going back to university to get a Ph.D. degree, be careful with the knowledge that you acquire. Much of it will be useless in the game of life. You will also discover that it's much harder to get rid of a Ph.D. than to acquire one!

25

Contrary to Popular Belief,
Time Is Not Money

In modern Western culture addicted to materialism, workaholism, and speed, the battle cry has become "Time is money." Contrary to this popular belief perpetuated by the business world, time is not money. Time is worth a lot more than money. Time is life. Time is also happiness.

Clearly, in today's fast-paced, stressed-out Western world, time is more precious than ever before. "Lost time," declared Benjamin Franklin, "is never found again." Time, in fact, is our scarcest resource. It is a finite resource on which we place infinite demands by trying to do too much with it.

Billionaire Nicolas Hayek, who reshaped the insolvent Swiss watch industry into a multi-billion dollar empire, had this to say about time: "Time is both wonderful and horrible. It is my work and life. Yet I hate time. Why? Because you cannot stop it. You cannot possess it. It's always present, but if you try to hold it, it disappears. And don't try to use personal tricks to fool time. It will always catch up with you."

If you want to have time on your side, you can't be fighting it. Indeed, to fight time is as asinine as to fight the law of gravity and the Easy Rule of Life. Together, the three will sooner or later — likely sooner than later — put you six feet under. There is no better evidence that you are fighting time than the fact you are always hurried. Always feeling rushed is no way to live for a prosperity-minded individual.

To be sure, the objective of life is not to get through it as fast as possible. Perhaps you aren't concerned about the rapid pace of your life. The thing you should be concerned about, however, is the abrupt stop at the end of it — much earlier than you expected. And you are going to reach the end of life at a much younger age if you don't learn to slow down.

Your mind can be your greatest asset, but it can play tricks on you. One such nasty trick is it makes you believe that you don't have sufficient time to do your work and still have time to lead a satisfying, balanced lifestyle that includes time for relaxation, social engagements, and other leisure activities. Perhaps you should think again! You have 1,440 minutes or 86,400 seconds in a day. That's the same amount of time that everyone else on Earth has, including people who have a full, relaxed, happy, and satisfying lifestyle.

Putting more time in your life is actually quite easy. Whenever you are short on time for the good things in life, you must create more time by making better use of it. A recent research study at Penn State University indicated that what we perceive as a time crunch in large measure is just erroneous perception. We all have enough time to do the important and enjoyable things, but we squander it. If we would make excellent use of just 30 or 40 percent of our time, we wouldn't have any shortage.

Other studies indicate that due to fewer children and less housework, the majority of North Americans have more free time now — about five hours a week — than in the recent past. The problem is not one of insufficient leisure time. Free time is available, but most North Americans waste it watching television and pursuing other useless activities.

Most of us spend our lives as if we had another life to draw on in the future when this one runs out. Unfortunately, the clock is always running. Indeed, time stops for no one. Time doesn't care whether you waste it or use it wisely. Time just keeps rolling merrily along. It's up to you to make sure that you don't waste your life away.

You must make time work for you and not against you. Live your life according to the motto "time is happiness" or "time is life" instead of "time is money," and you will show the world that you truly know the value of time. After all, you can't earn more time regardless of how hard you work. Just as important, you can't buy more time no matter how much money you have. So spend your time wisely — much more so than money.

26

Slow Down and the Rest of the World Will Slow Down for You

One of the realities of modern life is that we all have many things we would like to pursue — but limited time for pursuing them. We have to make decisions as to how we spend our time, not only in how much we work, but also in how we utilize our leisure time. Irrespective of our income and net worth, we can be truly prosperous only if we have a good balance between work and play.

It may appear that the most effective way to put more time in your life is to rush more during the day and try to do as many things as possible in the shortest possible time. Perhaps you have tried this many times and discovered that you always feel even more time deprived. No wonder that an old Dutch proverb contends, "The hurrier we go, the behinder we get."

Truth be known, squeezing as many leisure activities as possible into your personal time won't help you attain a balanced and relaxed lifestyle. Ironically, the activities that are supposed to help you relieve stress and enhance your health can actually have the opposite effect if you try to rush through them. Exercising in a hurry, for example, is liable to create more stress than it dissipates. In the same vein, you can't meditate effectively if you feel rushed. You are likely to regret having meditated at all when you realize you have wasted your time.

In the corporate environment, time management is frequently touted as the way to control time and put more of it into our lives. Classical time management doesn't work, however, because it supports trying to do more and more in a limited amount of time. The problem with using traditional time-management techniques is that you will still be dedicating a lot of your effort and time into things that are unimportant. You will still spend ten or twelve hours a day working at your job when you should be spending a maximum of eight.

Instead of managing time, you must transcend it. In simple terms, the object is to put more time into your life so that you are able to do your own thing at your own speed. The key is to forget about what the masses are doing. Even if practically everyone else seems to increase the pace of life every day, you don't have to try to keep up. You must take control of your physical and psychic space instead of allowing the distractions of the modern world to influence your lifestyle.

The peak performer's key to mastering time may surprise you: To make your days longer, don't rush; slow down instead. Adopt this principle and in a somewhat magical way you will have more time in your life. Once you slow down, you will no longer fight time; you will master it. Being totally involved in any activity, whether writing your first novel, walking in the park, talking to your neighbor, or taking a shower, will make the whole world slow down for you.

The next time you think that you don't have time to enjoy a sunset, think about it a little more. Clearly, the most important time to enjoy a sunset is when you don't have time for it. Taking ten minutes to watch the sun go down will do more to help you catch up with the world than rushing around for several hours.

The more sunsets you stop to enjoy, the more relaxed and less rushed life will be. Moreover, you will realize the importance of reducing the number of planned activities so that you get more quality in those few that you pursue.

Needless to say, there is no obligation on your part to apologize to anyone for slowing down and enjoying life. If someone asks what has gotten into you, tell them that you recently read the international bestseller *The Joy of Not Working* and agreed with every word in the book. Not everyone will approve of your behavior — but this will add to your satisfaction and enjoyment of life.

27

A Good Friend Is Much Cheaper than Therapy — and Ten Times As Helpful!

"People report being happier when they are with friends than when they're with a spouse or child," according to research cited in a recent cover story in *Psychology Today* magazine. This, indeed, is something to ponder seriously. To repeat, people actually experience greater joy while spending time with their friends than while spending time with their children or their mates. This should give you an idea of the value of friendship.

Interestingly, friendship is one of the most researched subjects on the Internet. This indicates that millions of people are interested in creating new friendships and enhancing old ones. Given how important friendship is in our lives, have you ever noticed how little has been written on the subject? Compare, for example, the number of books written on how to handle money to the number of books on how to create and maintain great friends.

Yet in many ways friendship is much more valuable to us than money. Indeed, our human interactions, particularly those with close friends, provide most of the joys or disappointments we have in life. It follows that you can't experience real success in life unless you have real friends.

Taking into account that passing time with friends provides us with so much joy and happiness, the question you have to ask yourself is, "Do I have enough close friends?" According to a study reported in the June 2006 issue of *American Sociological Review*, American adults, who shocked pollsters in 1985 when they said they had only three close friends, said they had just two in 2006. Moreover, the number who said that they have no one to discuss important matters with has doubled to one in four. The study found that men and women of every race, age, and education level reported fewer intimate friends than a similar survey indicated in 1985.

Unfortunately, the modern work world makes our individual lives busier and more fragmented. Thus, many people neglect to devote time to making close friends. "Friendship seems to be the last thing that anyone's getting to," says Jan Yager, an American sociologist and author of several books on friendship.

Yager adds, "Friendship is not something that you get to when everything else in your life is taken care of. It's an important relationship even after the school years for emotional health, for career advancement, for physical well-being." Great friendships are important for creating a new sense of community that translates into social, emotional, and physical well-being. Several research studies conclude that people who have intimate relationships with others live happier, healthier, and longer.

Friendship should be a universal and all-encompassing topic for each and every one of us. Companionship is essential to a full and rich life. It ranks right up there with fulfilling work and good health. Many individuals have discovered that a good friend is much cheaper than therapy — and ten times as helpful!

People in our society likely do not speak often about their yearning for friendship, as important as it is, because they do not want to appear needy and desperate. Not many people care to admit how lonely they are or can be at times in their lives. Surveys reveal that loneliness is one of the biggest problems humans face. To many people, it is the biggest.

Of this you should be certain: Life can be a really lonely experience without great friends. Above all, great friends can provide you with things that you can't. The reverse is also true. Plautus, the Roman playwright whose works influenced Shakespeare and Molière, proclaimed, "Your wealth is where your friends are."

Put another way, the more people who truly care whether you get up in the morning, the richer you will feel. You will find this to be true whether you are wealthy or broke. Taking into account the importance of friendship in our lives, the richest person in this world is the one with the most real friends — and not the one with the most money.

28

Ten Million Dollars Cannot Buy
What Great Friendship Can

Although we may not realize it at the time, a chief event in our lives is the day in which we first encounter one of our best friends. If by chance you don't precisely know why you need great friends, let's get you started: After you work either hard or smart to be successful in life, it's important to enjoy your success. Celebrations by yourself, you may have noticed, aren't much fun — they actually tend to be on the quiet side. Even if you have a dog or cat, sharing good news with it isn't quite the same as sharing good news with a great friend.

All things considered, happiness is one of the cheapest things in the world when we secure a good part of it through friendship. Portland resident Lenny Dee told an *Utne Reader* reporter, "I have always thought you could invest your energies in making money or making friends. And they achieve much the same ends — security, new experiences, personal options, travel, and so forth. I have always found it more fulfilling to make friends."

Money contributes to our lives, without doubt, but it's just that friendship contributes a lot more. At this point it is worth asking: Can true friends be bought? Not with money — luckily so for the happy poor and unfortunately for the lonely rich. "A friend you have to buy," declared George D. Prentice, "won't be worth what you pay for him."

Even so, friends have to be bought. To be sure, friendship carries a price tag — a big one at that. Hey, it should — it is one of life's greatest joys! To find, win, and keep great friends, you must continually be paying a price. Although many people are not wild about having to continually pay a price for anything, that's just the way it is. The Universe has declared that this is how the friendship game is played.

The price you have to pay for friendship varies in substance and form. Most important, you buy great friendship with intangible substance. You buy great friendship with the inspiration, advice, joy, support, and good feelings that friends expect from you. The major friendship maxim is that the best friends that money can buy will never even come close in quality to the friends that your character, integrity, and compassion will get you.

No doubt friendship is not always easy — you may have to put in a lot of time and effort for it to work. To have a true friend is one of the highest prizes of life. To be a true friend in return is one of the most formidable tasks in life. In this regard, always remember that friendship is a verb and not a noun. Put another way, friendship is an active element that requires constant input for it to develop, survive, and thrive.

Whatever you do, don't expect something for nothing. Friendship doesn't work that way. At times, particularly when growing new friendships, you may even have to put more into them than you get out. But the rewards of paying the price to develop great friends can bring prizes of which you have never dreamt.

Perhaps you have noticed that attention and kindness from a true friend will warm your heart a lot more when you are sick than receiving $1,000 from a distant or crabby relative. To be sure, your best support during troubled times will always be a dear friend. According to an old Greek proverb, "It is better in times of need to have a friend rather than money." In fact, a great friend is someone with whom you can have fun even when neither of you has any money.

At this point it is worth remembering that friendship isn't important only when you are in dire need. Without great friends, a journey to an exotic foreign land can be boring; a million dollars will not have much use; Christmas Day will be lousy; the most important of your accomplishments may appear worthless; and life, itself, will not even come close to being as precious and fulfilling.

29

One True Friend Is Worth More than 10,000 Superficial Ones

Again, there aren't many things on this planet that are more precious that true friends. It was the Greek writer Euripides who said, "One loyal friend is worth 10,000 relatives." Fortunately, we get to choose our friends as opposed to relatives, who are forced upon us.

When choosing new friends, however, much care should be taken. The key to optimizing happiness is to cultivate quality friendships with a few happy and interesting individuals. Quality is more important than quantity. In this regard, we can rephrase the above words of Euripides to "One true friend is worth more than 10,000 superficial ones."

As in many areas of life, less can be more in the friendship game. Although it's nice to have a lot of friends, too many will complicate your life. Succumbing to the temptation to have as many friends as possible will hinder your overall happiness, since it depletes your time, energy, money, and creativity — resources that can be better utilized in getting whatever else you want out of life. What's more, it's unlikely that you will develop many real friends if you spread yourself too thin among too many individuals.

Being popular — if that is what you desire — will not contribute much to how many true friends you acquire in your lifetime. In the truest sense, friendship is based on relationships that are held together by trust, respect, and mutual admiration. If you feel the need to be one of the girls or boys just to be popular, it is best that you head back to junior high and play the superficial games that teenyboppers play. Clearly, you need to be more developed and mature to play the adult friendship game.

Never feel bad about being unpopular with many people. This doesn't mean that you can't have friends. Socrates was unpopular. Freud was unpopular. Jesus was unpopular. Get the point? The point is that all of them still had friends.

It's just as important to put popularity in its proper place when you are looking for a friend. The fact that a person is popular doesn't mean that he or she will make a great friend. "A friend to all," warned Aristotle, "is a friend to none." Some individuals are not popular because they are different and don't fit in with the "me-too" crowd, whose members tend to imitate each other and aren't quite sure whom exactly they are trying to imitate.

Fact is, many genuine — but different — people are unpopular because peculiarity breeds contempt in our society. Yet it has been my experience that some of these unpopular people can make great friends. I would rather hang around genuine, different individuals who offend a lot of people than trendy me-too people who all talk and look alike and don't seem to offend anyone but me. My contention is that it is better to wind up with three or four true and genuine friends than twenty-five pseudo-friends who will not go out of their way to make time for you or will not help make you a better person.

All things considered, true friends add to your happiness and seldom, if ever, subtract from it. As Pulitzer Prize winner Alice Walker concluded, "No person is your friend (or kin) who demands your silence, or denies your right to grow and be perceived as fully blossomed as you were intended." Try surrounding yourself with people who radiate warmth, kindness, and a fresh perspective on life in general. You are likely to wind up with at least one true friend.

In my view, a true friend is also someone with whom you can do something boring — and still enjoy it. Most important, a true friend should remind you of the person you would like to be. Perhaps you haven't found "the real thing" in the way of friends. Thus the words of philosopher Ralph Waldo Emerson: "The only way to have a friend, is to be one."

This brings up an important question: Just what kind of friend are you? Generate a list of the important qualities you would like in a friend. These are the same ones that you should develop and maintain if you want to attract quality friends into your life. In short, do the things that will make you the sort of person you yourself would really want to hang out with.

30

If You Can Be Happy Only with Others — and Not Alone — You Are Not a Very Happy Person

Throughout the ages many accomplished individuals have sung the praises of being alone. Henry David Thoreau, for instance, boasted, "I find it wholesome to be alone the greater part of the time. To be in company, even with the best, is soon wearisome and dissipating. I love to be alone. I never found the companion that was so companionable as solitude."

This leads into the all-important question: Can you enjoy spending a lot of time alone? If you can't, it's likely a sign that you aren't able to discover quality in your own character. Put another way, you have low self-esteem, a sense of feeling unworthy and undeserving of your own company. Of course, not liking yourself can be a giant barrier to enjoying life in general.

If you want to master the art of being happy while alone, you must come to terms with the fact that aloneness is not synonymous with loneliness. There are two sides to being alone. The painful side is loneliness, which leads to symptoms associated with boredom, such as anxiousness and unhappiness. These can further lead to ailments such as headaches, excessive sleeping, insomnia, and depression. At the extreme, people commit suicide.

The other side to being alone is the pleasant side — best known as solitude. Solitude is an opportunity to indulge in many delightful activities that can only be enjoyed alone. Although loneliness can mean dejection and sadness, solitude can mean contentment and even ecstasy. "Solitude makes us tougher towards ourselves and tenderer towards others," according to Friedrich Nietzsche. "In both ways it improves our character."

Sadly, most people never discover the pleasant side to being alone and the rewards it brings us. Some people always feel alone, even in a crowd of people. Many lonely people turn to others for validation, not realizing that true validation can only come from within. For this reason, Russian writer Anton Chekhov warned, "If you are afraid of loneliness, do not marry."

All things considered, if you can only be happy with other people — and not alone — you are not a very happy person. Loneliness when you are with others is a lack of connectedness with others. Similarly, loneliness when you are alone is a lack of connectedness with yourself. Incidentally, if you don't like yourself, why would you expect anyone else to like you?

To overcome loneliness, we must learn how to spend our time alone creatively. The majority of us flee to society — as dull as society is most of the time — searching for some excitement to escape the greater dullness inside ourselves. We also flee to society because we fear being alone. Yet many of us end up feeling lonelier in a crowd than we are by ourselves.

There are two ways to react when you feel lonely while alone. One response is known as sad passivity. This includes crying, moping, excess eating, sleeping, and feeling sorry for yourself. This reaction is normally the result of low self-esteem and a lack of defined goals for handling aloneness.

Other unhealthy ways to handle loneliness are getting stoned, boozing, gambling, and shopping. In the short term, these seem to help alleviate loneliness. In the long run, however, they don't enhance social skills, help form close relationships, or develop high self-esteem.

The other response to loneliness is creative action. This should include solo activities such as reading, writing letters, studying, listening to music, working on a hobby, playing a musical instrument, and meditating. You will find that being alone is a process of self-development, self-discovery, and self-love. What's more, learning to like spending time by yourself will heighten the fun you have when you are with your friends.

For this reason, don't enjoy solitude only when it is forced upon you; seek it when it isn't. You will learn to love yourself while getting to know yourself better. When you learn to enjoy your own company, you will discover the paradise you have been looking for and all the happiness you will ever need.

31

People Are Only Human — If They Weren't, Life Would Be Different

We all have to deal with them on a daily basis: weird and difficult people. At times of frustration and disappointment with these characters, a friend of mine mutters, "Human beings, what a stupid concept!" Mark Twain must have felt the same when he wrote, "If man had created man he would be ashamed of his performance."

Like my friend, you probably sometimes wish that other human beings — especially those with whom you live and work — were as logical, trustworthy, intelligent, kind, hard-working, fun-loving, and practical as you. In fact, you want to help thousands of people to be a lot less dysfunctional so that they can be more like you. No doubt the world would be a much better place.

Are you wrong in saying that so many human beings can be quite ignorant? Apparently not. Albert Einstein must have been generally disappointed with people when he wrote, "Only two things are infinite, the universe and human stupidity, and I'm not sure about the former." Frank Dane concurred with his classic statement: "Ignorance is never out of style. It was in fashion yesterday, it is the rage today, and it will set the pace tomorrow."

Granted, there are a lot of ignorant human beings out there. But are all these ignorant people bad human beings or are they just different from you and me? At this point it is also worth asking: Are our unreasonable expectations of other people contributing to the ignorance and other flaws we see in them? Given that other people are not perfect, it's best that we accept them as they are or else fall victim to their whims.

You will inevitably find that many people will hurt you in the event you let them. Certain critics will try to burst your bubble and knock you off your cloud. They will try to interfere with your plans and projects even when they have no direct interest in them. Irrespective of how much good you do on a project, someone, somewhere, will find reasons to complain about your performance. While you are trying to light the fire in your life, someone will try to put it out for you.

There are many more frustrating human traits. Friends and relatives will let you down, even though you have just performed several special favors for them. You will find that many people don't play by the same rules as you. Some will drive you crazy because they change their minds from one minute to the next. You and I agree that there are even certain people on this planet who probably shouldn't be here.

But keep in mind that the roles are often reversed. You are also human and you will occasionally, or even frequently, let other people down. You will screw up and you will do dumb things and you will upset others. You won't meet someone else's high standards regardless of how hard you work at it. You will also criticize and reject other people, and potentially create the same effect on others as people who criticize and reject you have had on you.

You can accept that rocks are hard and water is wet. Then make allowances for the fact that people are only human. To be sure, if they weren't, life would be different. But with all the negative traits that humans tend to exhibit, they are still an important element in the happiness game. Human nature is fickle or outrageous at times. No doubt many people can be more dishonest, rude, unreasonable, inconsiderate, and ignorant than you. Just don't freak out when they are.

The key to making people more pleasurable is to be less offended by human nature. Focus more on people's positive qualities than the negative. Viewed in this way, humans can be accommodating, generous, inspiring, humorous, gentle, charitable, and forgiving. In the midst of it all, spend a lot less time judging the human race. You have more important things to do with your life. Judging others is tedious and won't make you many friends — besides, the last time I checked, judging other people was still God's job.

32

It's All Too Easy to Overestimate Your Ability to Change Others

Common sense tells us that we shouldn't waste time on things that we can't change. This applies, not just to situations and events, but to people as well. Yet all of us fall into the trap of trying to change people to the way we would like them to be. If you fall into this trap yourself, you should question whether it's wise to try to transform others. Everything can make perfectly good sense if you never really think about it all that much — but sometimes you must.

Fact is, it's all too easy to overestimate your ability to change others. This includes friends, relatives, lovers, and neurotics. Before you try to transform people into better human beings, first there is the issue of whether you should be trying to change them at all. Perhaps you are trying to reshape someone for "his or her own good." Clearly, this is only a superficial rationalization for your attempts to manipulate someone to be like you would like him or her to be.

It is not your duty to perform the psychological brain surgery that may be necessary for certain people to be happy or successful in life. You should respect the fact that people have a right to live their own lives the way they choose. You may find a certain person's way of life disgusting, but he or she may think your way of life is even more disgusting. So, who is right? Perhaps both of you are.

But so what? It doesn't matter who is right. As long as a particular lifestyle is neither illegal nor physically harmful to anyone, the person living it should be left alone. Trying to change others is sometimes motivated by an erroneous belief that others should be doing things the way you would do them. Your way may be the right way and it may not. What's more, even if your way is right, there may be more than one right way.

Perhaps, like disgraced former U.S. President Richard Nixon, you are convinced that you would have made a good pope. No doubt anyone with as much moral authority as you would put the present pope to shame. This still doesn't give you the right to try to change anyone. It's foolish to think that God expects anyone to interfere in other people's lives as some act of divine intervention. You may have high standards, but who is to say that everyone should be meeting them? If people don't meet your standards, why try to change them? Spend less time with these individuals. Seek out those people who meet your standards and don't need any guidance from you.

You may still feel inclined toward riding to the rescue of individuals who are facing major difficulties in their lives. It's easy to fall into the temptation to try to change certain individuals — to have them be more motivated, more organized, more reasonable, or more trustworthy. But you must resist because it's a mistake to try to change negative people — to expect their imminent transformation into more positive individuals. Your efforts will be futile.

You can give your sermon on the four corners of this planet to your heart's content. Yet nobody is going to care if it doesn't fit in with their own philosophy. How right Richard Bach was when he wrote, "No one can solve problems for someone whose problem is that they don't want their problems solved." Generally speaking, negative people don't want to change; if they do change, it is only after a lengthy period — time you can't afford to lose.

In the same vein, don't make the mistake of trying to change friends or relatives. The worst mistake you can make is marrying someone in the hope that you can influence him or her to change sooner or later. Nothing is more frustrating than being in love with someone who is not what you would like him or her to be. Most people are unwilling to change — even over the long term. The ones who are will do it on their own terms and only when they are ready. People change only if they want to change, and when left to their own devices.

All things considered, we really can't ever change anyone but ourselves. Trying to change someone else's ways will be a total waste of your precious time. The wise thing to do is to mind your own business and spend that precious time changing yourself for the better. Do keep in mind that it takes all kinds of people to make an interesting and exciting world. Imagine how boring the world would be if everyone were exactly like you.

33

Giving Advice to Anyone Means That You Either Lose or Break Even

One day German poet Otto Erich Hartleben consulted a doctor about his health problems. The doctor advised Hartleben to quit smoking cigarettes and to stop drinking alcohol. The doctor added, "This visit will cost you three marks." "I'm not paying you," retorted Hartleben, "because I'm not taking your advice."

Undoubtedly, you have found this out through experience: Most people won't follow advice — regardless of how good it is — as was the case with poet Otto Erich Hartleben. Your advice may very well be helpful, but if it means that the recipient of the advice must put in some work and effort, he or she will likely discard it. Giving advice may not only be a waste of your time and energy — it can be dangerous as well.

It is particularly dangerous to offer advice when the person hasn't asked for it. Some people will refuse to take advice regardless of how good it is and how noble your intentions are. Your relationship with them can get strained to the limit if you persist. People may not realize that you are trying to help them. On the contrary, they may think that you are highly judgmental and are trying to make them wrong. Your advice is likely to be ignored because most people don't want to admit they are wrong.

Trying to solve other people's problems with your unsolicited advice is as futile as trying to change people. It's best not to get immersed in other people's problems, including those of your spouse, friends, and co-workers. Trying to solve their problems is tantamount to saying they aren't capable of doing it on their own. Benjamin Franklin may have given us the best advice possible about giving unsolicited advice: "Wise men don't need advice. Fools don't take it."

It may be dangerous to give advice even if it is solicited. The problem is the advice we give others may be the opposite of what they expect or desire. "When a man comes to me for advice," quipped Josh Billings, "I find out the kind of advice he wants, and I give it to him." Giving advice that people expect may be a good strategy at times, but it can be dangerous in certain situations. Taking into account that many people don't have a complete and sensible appreciation of their own predicaments, it follows that they may in fact expect advice that will end up hurting their cause.

Even giving good advice can get you in trouble — particularly when it involves the truth. Oscar Wilde wrote, "It is always silly to give advice, but to give good advice is absolutely fatal." There is a lot to be said about telling the truth — but telling the truth in many cases is on the first rung of the living-dangerously ladder.

For instance, whenever a friend asks you how she can improve the meal that she just cooked for you, it is wise not to mention the twenty things you would have done differently. Otherwise, you could end up without an opportunity to eat any more of the soufflé because you will be wearing it over the expensive shirt you wore for the first time.

All things considered, giving advice to anyone means that you either lose or break even. You seldom win. Whenever people accept your advice, and it turns out to be helpful, people likely won't acknowledge you for it. They may not even remember that you gave it to them. Whenever they accept your advice, and it turns out to be harmful, people won't forget who gave it to them. They will probably even resent you for having given them bad advice.

Summing up, it's best to avoid getting involved in people's personal affairs, especially if you haven't been asked. As a well-balanced individual you shouldn't need to inflate your ego by giving unsolicited advice. If you are going to give any, however, advise the person that it's best to avoid freely accepting advice from anyone else — and that includes you.

Whenever you feel compelled to respond to a request for advice, say it simply. Make it short. Don't rant and rave. Even so, on extremely sensitive matters, be sure to duck when flying objects start coming your way.

34
Don't Walk away from Negative People — Run!

We all have a negative acquaintance or two who seems to know everything there is to know about what is wrong with this world. These pessimistic individuals, to be sure, can be just a little unpleasant and difficult to be around. If you are like me, after a few moments with them, you begin to squirm in your seat, trying to determine your next course of action.

Unfortunately, there are no laws under which you can have negative people charged for interfering with your life. As a highly evolved human being, you will want to avoid being around pessimistic people, even if the alternative is being alone. It is important that you spot negative people as soon as possible so that you can take appropriate action.

Negative people will try to undermine your optimism in any way they can. They will bore you with bad tidings and gossip, continuing to tell you the negative things in their lives when you already know more about them than you care to know. If you hang around them for too long, they will influence you to start seeing nothing but a grim and gloomy world.

Pessimistic individuals think the whole world is against them. For some strange reason they want everyone else to have the same experience. They are critics who know everything — at least they think they do. Pessimistic people court others who will support them in their contention that the world is a lousy place. And once they know they can, they will stick to them like Krazy Glue® to hair. Some of these people spend their entire lives making others miserable. They seem to be pleased with their efforts for no justifiable reason.

Negative people are particularly noted for their lack of humor. They have the delightful view that life is a rip-off and that nothing is so bad that it can't get worse. One of the most endearing traits of pessimistic people is their willingness to do anything possible to bring optimistic people down to their depressing level. Indeed, misery doesn't only love company — it demands it! These people have an endless supply of hard-luck stories capable of bringing down even the most enthusiastic and energetic people.

You may think that you can convince negative people to be remarkably positive like you. Reality says you probably won't win many converts irrespective of how much effort you put into this experiment. Nothing irks negative and unsuccessful people more than individuals who are positive and successful. Accept that some people prefer to look at the world from a perversely distorted point of view.

Perhaps you are a Good Samaritan who likes to take on one or two neurotics as a personal project. I must warn you about the futility of this venture. Unless you can get these people to have personality transplants, all your efforts will be in vain. Even if their happiness and survival are at stake, negative individuals won't change. Although they have the ability to change, they go on defending their points of view at all costs while looking for new converts.

As a matter of course, negative people will intrude into your life every chance they get. You have to be able to stop them before they get started. Some will claim you owe them some of your time; others will claim you owe them favors; and still others will even claim you owe them a living.

In short, it is futile to spend your time trying to make an unhappy person happy. Near as I can tell, you'd have to be a magician to pull it off. There is only one way to effectively deal with negative people — eliminate them from your life. Try to direct them in one direction while you head off in the opposite one. If you somehow find yourself in the company of someone who regularly drains your energy, it's wise not to stick around. Look for any means of rapid escape. In other words, don't walk away from negative people — run!

To be fair, negative people are just ignorant and don't know any better. What's more, they are not complete failures — we get to use them as great examples of the type of people we don't want to become ourselves.

35

If You Hang Around with a Bunch of Blunderers Long Enough, You Will Become One Yourself

To get the most out of your companionship, you must choose your friends well. One of the greatest time-wasters and obstacles to success in all areas of life is associating with the wrong people. Yet surprisingly many individuals spend time with dysfunctional characters whom they don't even like. Associating with the wrong people can cost you your time, energy, creativity, and money. They can even cost you your health — mainly mental.

To achieve success in your career and personal life, it helps to have friends who are going to inspire you to greater heights. "Keep away from people who try to belittle your ambitions," advised Mark Twain. "Small people always do that, but the really great make you feel that you, too, can become great." In other words, the people closest to you will either keep you down or help you up. You want to hang around a group of motivated people with whom you can trade ideas, find inspiration, and not end up dejected every time you meet with them.

It is a terrible mistake to befriend a bunch of misfits solely because it makes you look like a genius whenever you are around them. After all is said — and mostly left undone — there is no glory in outdoing a bunch of muddleheads and blunderers. If you hang around with a bunch of misfits, you are likely to become one yourself. Just like them, you will come back from the Burger King with ketchup on your shirt after eating two more hamburgers than you should have.

Sure, negative people can come in handy if you are negative yourself. If you consult enough negative people, you can confirm any negative opinion you have of something or someone else. But being a skeptic is not in itself a virtue. What good is it to mix with negative people who are going to pump you up with negative energy and negative beliefs? If you are like me, you have enough of your own negativity that you have to continually conquer.

The best strategy is to avoid endarkened people at all costs — hang around with enlightened people instead. Stay away from people who set low personal standards that they constantly fail to achieve. Make friends, instead, with individuals who have big dreams for themselves. Associate with people who are making it in life, not ones who are barely hanging on. The former are much harder to find than the latter, but when you find them, the price you will have paid will be well worth it.

Generally speaking, birds of a feather flock together. So if you want to soar with the eagles, don't hang around with the turkeys. Hang around with a bunch of blunderers long enough and you will become one yourself. As you can well imagine, it's difficult to be successful if you are constantly distracted by fools. What's more, associate with just one loser and soon there will be more. Surprisingly, you wouldn't think that losers can multiply, but they can.

If we force ourselves into constant contact with "cool and creative," the odds are sky-high that cool and creative will wear off on us. Hang out with cool and creative Web designers, for instance, and you will end up cool and creative. Ditto: Cool and creative life coaches. Ditto: Cool and creative janitors. Ditto: Cool and creative engineers (granted, having been an engineer in a former life, I realize that I may be stretching it here). The point is that a part of you becomes whom you hang with. No doubt your parents warned you that you shouldn't associate with fools or losers. They were right, weren't they?

It behooves every one of us to adopt the wisdom of Joseph Marshall Wade: "If I wanted to become a tramp, I would seek information and advice from the most successful tramp I could find," wrote Wade. "If I wanted to become a failure, I would seek advice from men who have never succeeded. If I wanted to succeed in all things, I would look around me for those who are succeeding, and do as they have done."

Thus, drink coffee only with positive, focused people who will teach you a lot and who will not drain your valuable energy with their constant complaining and lousy attitudes. By developing relationships with individuals committed to constant improvement and the pursuit of the best that life has to offer, you will have plenty of company on your path to the top of whatever mountain you seek to climb.

36

There's Insanity on Both Sides of the Debate When You Argue with an Idiot

It's somewhat of an understatement when I say that many people love to argue, that arguing is their favorite pastime. These neurotics are willing to partake in any dispute. By engaging you in a verbal battle, they get a chance to discredit your ideas and beliefs. Some desperate people will even argue about absolutely nothing just for the sake of arguing and trying to win a debate. At some point — likely much too late — you will realize how unreasonable these people are if you take their bait. Fact is, argumentative people will run you completely off your rails if you allow them.

You yourself may love debating issues but you must realize that your life is much too short to waste on frivolous arguments, even with friends, relatives, and your spouse. Plain and simple, arguing over trivial matters wastes time and energy that could be utilized doing some real living. Just as important, perhaps, is the fact that it's not worth getting involved in an argument that you can't win.

Whenever you catch yourself arguing with a friend or relative, ask yourself where the argument may lead. What is the payoff? If you must make a point, make it and leave it at that. You probably won't succeed in changing the opinion of most people, regardless of how relevant your facts are, and how well you argue your case.

How about when you definitely know that you are right, and someone else is terribly wrong, in an important matter that can affect the person's health or financial well-being? The problem is that with certain individuals, the more you try to influence their thinking, the more they will resist. To oppose unreasonable people is to encourage them. Leave them alone. Often it is best to let people learn for themselves what they are doing wrong. People will learn faster by making their own mistakes. As Josh Billings once proclaimed, "The best way to convince a fool he is wrong is to let him have his way."

Wasting time on arguments with friends, relatives, and spouses is one thing. We have to seriously question our own sanity, however, when we find ourselves debating with someone whose favorite pastime is arguing. Plain and simple, some people are just opposition looking for something to oppose — opposition is where they are coming from and opposition is where they are headed. You will find your beliefs under attack regardless of what you believe. Whatever side you take, they will argue the opposite.

If their view of life is radically different from yours, it gets worse. The more you poke holes in their arguments, the more unreasonable they become. Irrespective of the many facts you present to support your position, they will be oblivious to them. Truth and logic don't matter to them. People who love to argue will zealously promote useless ideas, defend poor reasoning, and defy clarity. They will never change their tune regardless of how much overwhelming evidence you have to offer.

Of the many principles for dealing with argumentative individuals, these four stand out: (1) Anything worth arguing about is probably worth avoiding even more. (2) You can't outtalk people who don't know what they — or you — are talking about. (3) An argument carried far enough will make it totally worthless. (4) No one ever won an argument that lost a friend.

Clearly, whenever you find yourself in a ridiculous argument, it's best to get out of it immediately. You may be tempted to get worked up about it, or even throw a temper tantrum. Don't take the bait. Allowing someone to make you angry is allowing him or her to control you. An effective way to get rid of an argument addict is to ignore the person. Keep your cool and be on your merry way. The best overall response is to avoid the neurotics who love to argue.

The next time you are tempted to get involved in a debate with an irrational person, ask yourself why you would want to convert an idiot to your cause. What's more, it's important to respect the First Law of Debate as proposed by Arthur Bloch: "Never argue with a fool — people may not know the difference." Allow me to put this another way: There's insanity on both sides of the debate when you argue with an idiot.

37

The Best Way to Impress Other People Is by Not Trying to Impress Them

According to Samuel Johnson, "most people spend parts of their lives in attempts to display qualities they don't have." Indeed, motivated by the desire to be popular, many human beings go out of their way to impress the world with their nonexistent qualities. They may use expensive clothing, flashy cars, big houses, the latest fads, name-dropping, and past achievements in attempts to claim attention from other individuals.

Because we are social animals, the desire to be liked and respected is natural. In fact, whether we admit it or not, being endeared to others is incredibly important to just about everybody. If we are looking to associate with people of good character, however, displaying qualities that we don't have isn't the key to being more lovable.

No one impresses individuals with great character less than superficial people who go out of their way to try and impress others. The irony is that the best way to impress other people is by not trying to impress them. Well-balanced people are drawn to others who have inner confidence and don't have to seek approval.

To be sure, it's nice to be recognized for your achievements. The drawback is that trying to prove yourself to others by boasting and pointing out your accomplishments takes a lot of energy. The people who most count in your work life — those who can unlock doors and create opportunities for financial and career success — won't be influenced at all when it's obvious you are desperately trying to impress them. Just as important, perhaps, is that people in your personal life will start avoiding you if you spend too much time boasting about yourself.

It is just as futile to try to arouse others with your beauty, wealth, and power as with your achievements. You have to ask yourself, "What sort of people are going to be impressed by these things?" Probably not anyone with whom you can enjoy meaningful and enjoyable interactions. Besides, anyone worth knowing will discover your true qualities sooner or later — particularly once they realize that they have been sold a false bill of goods.

Plain and simple, you are setting yourself up for more problems in your life when you try to be something or someone you aren't. Anything that you say or do may reflect badly on your character. Anyone who longs to be somebody other than the person she is shows to others that she is miserable. When you are truly successful in this game called life, you have nothing to prove to anyone.

There is no need to drive an expensive car, live in a big house, or wear fashionable clothes in an attempt to be liked by others. The best alternative to trying to impress others is to be yourself. You must project who you really are instead of some act or facade that isn't you.

Stop caring about what others think of you. Completely! Totally! 100 percent! You will save yourself a lot of frustration and embarrassment. Heed the words of William Shakespeare: "This above all: to thine own self be true." This way you get respect and adulation to flow naturally to you.

Fact is, sharing your true self with others is usually a wonderful and fulfilling experience. When you are meeting people, the key is not to be desperate. The least amount of affection is going to flow your way when you seek it the most. The secret is to learn to relax, enjoy yourself, and be yourself. People of great character will always determine the quality of your personality by what you stand for, what you fight for, and what you live for.

Perhaps you would like to impress the whole world. Then spend your time making a positive difference in this world and the world will be impressed. I can give no better example than Mother Teresa.

The paradox is that your popularity has a much greater chance of hitting new heights when you don't actively seek popularity. How much you actually impress people will be directly proportional to how much you share your true self with them — and inversely proportional to how much you go out of your way to try to impress them.

38

Nice People Are Often Not Good People and Good People Are Often Not Nice People

We live in a culture in which being a nice person is considered tantamount to being a good person. The result is that many nice people are mistaken for fine human beings, when, in fact, they haven't earned this distinction due to their serious character defects. On the other hand, many really good people are mistaken for having serious character defects just because they aren't the nicest people around. So what makes a good person? "A good head and a good heart," Nelson Mandela reminded us, "are always a formidable combination."

No doubt at times it's hard for a lot of us to differentiate between the good guys and the bad guys. A friend of mine, for instance, is not the nicest person in the eyes of his friends and acquaintances. He is direct and often upsets others by telling the truth about events, people, and things. Yet my friend is one of the most generous individuals when it comes to giving money or other help to friends, panhandlers, and other people in need. Contrast this with many so-called nice people who seldom go out of their way to help others — particularly those in need.

The reality that nice people often are not good people and good people often are not nice people is a major disconnect for many of us. We want everyone to be nice because this is a lot easier to take than having people be direct, rude, or angry with us. Fact is, niceness is a facade that many individuals lacking exemplary character use for ulterior motives. Some of the nicest-appearing people are desperate for affection from others. Certain psychiatrists and psychologists claim that behind the nice-guy facade there usually lurks considerable repressed anger — waiting to be transformed into despicable acts against others.

The core of the matter is that we have to be on guard with many nice people. We can allow them to get by on charisma for only so long. After that, they better show some endearing character traits. Clearly, many people are nice so that they can distract us to take advantage of us. They will try to get in front of us in a lineup or entice us into the biggest scam the world has ever seen. People seeking to con others out of money or anything else invariably project themselves as a model of virtue. Your making a snap decision about their character based on their niceness can lead to serious consequences and disillusionment later on.

At the extreme are nice people who steal from senior citizens, commit sex crimes, or murder their relatives — not exactly the epitome of sterling character. How often have you heard others say, "He seemed so nice all the time," when describing someone who has just assaulted, or even killed, someone?

Good people, on the other hand, are not nice all the time. In his renowned study of self-actualized individuals, researcher and humanistic psychologist Abraham Maslow found that people at the highest level of psychological development aren't the most pleasant humans whom you will encounter. Self-actualized people aren't calm individuals. Indeed, temper outbursts are common.

Unlike nice people, self-actualized human beings can be constructively critical of others when the need is there. Because they don't pretend to be something they aren't, these good people aren't pleasing to everyone all of the time. Although they are generally very tolerant of others, self-actualized individuals are likely to create a big scene when people engage in insincerity, dishonesty, or stupidity.

If you want to surround yourself with human beings who possess great character, who will support you in making a difference in this world, don't overlook the good people just because they aren't nice all the time. Many good people have insecurities; they get angry and they may even get dejected about life. You will have to put up with their occasional anger, impatience, and disgust because they will not tolerate lying, cheating, inconsideration, or hypocrisy. Nonetheless, their honesty, sincerity, decency, goodness, wisdom, and consideration will make you realize that you are in great company.

39
Everyone in This World — Including You and Me — Is Selfish

As is to be expected, a large majority of individuals on this planet see themselves as a lot less selfish than the average individual. Upon close scrutiny, however, this doesn't make much sense. Provided it was possible to measure selfishness, about half of the people would be more selfish than the average person, and about half of the people would be less selfish. The point is, it is impossible for a large majority to be less selfish than the average person. There is no need to measure selfishness, however. Truth be known, everyone in this world — including you and me — is selfish.

Some people may have some difficulty with the idea that they are just as selfish as everyone else on this planet. We like to think there are selfless and selfish people on the two extremes. A lot of us would like others to think of us as being selfless instead of selfish. What's more, most of us — out of our own selfishness, I might add — would also like others to be less selfish.

Have you ever noticed that certain people will call you selfish, not for pursuing your own good, but for neglecting something that they want from you? There is a major disconnect here. The question is: Whenever they are calling you selfish in an attempt to get something from you, what is motivating them? Obviously, their motivation is none other than their own selfishness. Oscar Wilde articulated this point much more eloquently than I ever could with his classic statement: "Selfishness is not living as one wishes to live; it is asking others to live as one wishes to live."

Contrary to popular wisdom, whenever we do things for others, we are motivated by our selfishness. Some unknown wise person once defined altruism as "the art of doing unselfish things for selfish reasons." Put another way, we all are generous in a self-serving way.

For instance, I donate money to charities and the food bank out of selfishness and not selflessness. I make these donations because I want the world to work better. What's more, I feel good about giving to others. I am driven by my selfishness to have the world work better in the long term, at the expense of having less money for myself. There is nothing selfless about my generosity.

We can turn to the dictionary definitions of "selfish" and "selfless" to put this issue in proper perspective. "Selfless" is commonly defined as "Having, exhibiting, or motivated by no concern for oneself." Clearly, based on this definition, no one with a sane mind is selfless. Having no concern for oneself is a sign of severe mental illness — or rigor mortis. If we were selfless, we wouldn't snap up that great deal on the apartment or car or an item of clothing. We would say, "There are undoubtedly millions of people who need this more than I do. Since I am so caring and unselfish, I better leave it for one of them."

In the same vein, dictionaries commonly define "selfish" as "Concerned chiefly or only with oneself." Thus, everyone of sane mind on this planet must be selfish. The core of the matter is that, on some level or another, we are all concerned chiefly with ourselves. When we do things for others, we are ultimately doing those things for ourselves. Our motivation for performing good deeds for others can be to avoid guilt, to feel good about ourselves, to have others like us more, to make the world work better, or to get to Heaven.

Now don't freak out. Your selfishness is neither bad nor good. Accept it for what it is. Ensure that your selfishness is sensible and not irrational, however. Operating with the attitude "This is my world. This is all about me, myself, and I," will probably manifest itself as irrational selfishness when most people end up avoiding you.

In contrast, out of sensible selfishness, you can be kind, gentle, charitable, and considerate. Being a Good Samaritan will have a positive effect on your well-being. You will feel good about yourself, people of good character will want to be your friends, and the world will work better in the end. Best of all, you will likely wind up in Heaven.

40

When Someone Fails to Keep a Commitment, There Is a 95 Percent Chance That It Will Happen Again

A scorpion, who wants to get across a pond, spots a friendly frog. The scorpion says to the frog, "How about a lift to the other side of the pond? I can't swim and I would appreciate your helping me out." The frog replies, "No way. I know what scorpions are like. You promised not to sting me one time in the past when I gave you a lift. Yet you didn't keep your commitment and stung me. I almost died. This time you'll probably sting me halfway across the pond, from where I won't be able to swim to shore. I don't want to drown."

The scorpion counters, "Don't be silly. If I am on your back, I am dependent on you to get across the pond. If I sting you, I will drown too. Why would I want to do that?" The frog thinks a bit and relents: "I guess you're right. Hop on."

The scorpion climbs on the frog's back and they take off for the other side of the pond. Halfway across, the scorpion gives the frog a big whopper of a sting. As both of them start to go under, the frog says to the scorpion, "Why in the world did you do that? Why didn't you keep your commitment not to sting me? Now both of us are going to die." The scorpion's answer is one you have heard many times before from human scorpions: "I couldn't resist it. It's just my nature to be that way."

The lesson here is that if someone has failed to keep a commitment with you in the past, there is a 95 percent chance that he or she will fail to keep a commitment with you again in the future. This is a hard lesson for most of us to learn. In fact, many of us keep relearning this lesson throughout our entire lives.

You will notice that people who back out of business deals or social commitments tend to do it again and again and again. This behavior is best explained by two phenomena previously discussed — people are only human and people seldom change. Human nature is such that even if people have apologized for a past transgression, and promised that they wouldn't do it again, they will likely do it again. You have to decide what is the best way to respond to people who don't keep commitments.

Incidentally, the 95 percent chance that they will do it again applies even when they have offered an apology without your asking for one. When you have demanded an apology, and they have complied, then there is a 99 percent chance they will do it again. These are the same odds as when they haven't apologized.

The reason is that an apology demanded under some threat — such as you will terminate your friendship or business relationship if they don't apologize — is a form of blackmail. Put another way, an apology demanded from another person using some form of threat is never a true apology. The person may apologize for the transgression — but the apology is false. Fact is, a true apology — one that means something and comes from the heart — is made by a person without anyone else demanding it.

Personally, I refrain from dealing with people who regularly cop out of business or social commitments — whether or not they apologize. I don't need the hassles and aggravation. Whenever people continue to fail to show up for meetings, I don't contact them again. If they call to apologize with a good reason, I give them one more chance, and possibly two chances — but three strikes and they are out. By following this principle, without any exceptions, I end up with a few quality people who are good at keeping commitments.

In short, if a person has let you down before, be on guard when he tells you he will come through on another occasion. Whether it's a business deal or a social engagement, no matter how enticing and promising, it's best to focus your interests elsewhere. Otherwise, you will find out the hard way that the first transgression was no accident.

In fact, if you hang around him long enough, chances are fairly high that he will outdo his previous transgression with something so much worse that it makes the previous one seem insignificant. As the old saying goes, "The person who steals an egg from his farmer friend will eventually steal the chicken as well."

41

Good Deeds Are Seldom Remembered; Bad Deeds Are Seldom Forgotten

A fireman is lamenting his fate to an acquaintance at the bar. "One day I had to fight a house fire and I saved a family's two dogs. Do you think anyone remembers? Another time my colleagues and I suffered severe smoke inhalation saving an old church from severe damage. Not one person ever mentions this. I also risked my life entering a burning house to save three children. I almost died. Does anyone remember this? Not that I am aware of.

"But the only time I ever cursed and kicked a barking dog, it turned out to be the mayor's dog," continued the fireman. "Someone saw me do it and told everyone in town. Do you think anyone has forgotten this?"

The moral of this story is straightforward: Good deeds are seldom remembered and bad deeds are seldom forgotten. The ideal, of course, would be the converse. No such luck — reality intrudes again!

The key is to be realistic when you perform your act of kindness for someone. Don't expect anyone to remember your good deed forever. Self-delusion about the amount of payback you are going to receive from doing someone a great favor can lead to severe disappointment and dejection.

Besides, the fact that some good deeds aren't forgotten can be to your detriment. According to some unknown wise person, "If you help a friend in need, he is sure to remember you — the next time he is in need." In other words, be too generous and some people may look at your good deeds as their right — instead of a privilege for which they should be extremely grateful.

You should not avoid doing good deeds, however, simply because most of them will be forgotten and some of the ones remembered may be to your detriment. A good person performs many good deeds out of sheer selfishness — simply because the world works a whole lot better when people do great things for each other.

This issue may arise: Should you break your friendships when certain friends forget that you have performed more good deeds for them than they have done for you? Remember that even the best of friends have faults. "To find a friend one must close one eye. To keep him . . . two," according to British author Norman Douglas. Given that friends make life worth living, you may have to overlook the fact that certain friends don't perform as many acts of kindness for you as you perform for them.

The key to a happy and fulfilling life is not to focus all your time and energy on yourself. If you remain focused on how little people appreciate your good deeds, you are likely to become miserable. By all means, perform your act of kindness, but don't expect the recipient to remember it forever — regardless of how beneficial the act of kindness is to him or her.

"Act with kindness," Confucius told us, "but do not expect gratitude." The key is to have faith in the spiritual principle that when you do wonderful things for others, even more wonderful things will come back to you in the future when you least expect them.

Realistically, whenever you perform an act of kindness, don't expect the recipient's gratitude to last longer than the moment they say thank you. Not to say there aren't rare people who may remember the good deed for a long time. That's a bonus. Generally speaking, think of your good deeds as something you have done to make the world work better and to make yourself feel good about yourself. Forget your acts of kindness to others as quickly as possible, however — because most everyone else will.

42

The Surest Way to Failure Is Trying to Please Everyone

German philosopher Arthur Schopenhauer concluded that we forfeit three-fourths of ourselves to be like other people. One of the reasons we do this is to try to please everyone. As is to be expected, wanting respect and approval from others is natural for human beings. The problem isn't our desire for respect and approval from a few friends and acquaintances, however. What gets us in trouble is the desire to please the whole world.

"I cannot give you the formula for success," claimed American journalist Herbert Bayard Swope, "but I can give you the formula for failure which is: Try to please everybody." These words, indeed, are ones to ponder carefully. Way too many people squander most of their time and energy trying to please others instead of focusing on their own hopes, plans, and dreams. Don't be one of them.

The core of the matter is that applause, compliments, and praise are a bonus in life and shouldn't be a need. You can't be liked and praised by everyone you know. In fact, your ability to accept disapproval and rejection is a valuable trait that you should develop. After all, it is inevitable that you will encounter many people who will dislike you. Put another way, you can't please all of the people all of the time; you can't please any one person all of the time; and you can never please certain people any time.

Contrary to popular belief, there is nothing wrong with having made an enemy or two. "If you have no enemies, you are apt to be in the same predicament in regards to friends," advised American author Elbert Hubbard.

On the same note, famous humanistic psychologist Abraham Maslow found that individuals on the highest level of psychological development are willing to make enemies while they do what is right for themselves and the world. They realize that they can't please everyone, regardless of how talented they are and how hard they try. The desire to be liked by everyone is just another form of greed — and self-actualized people aren't greedy individuals.

If you want to make your mark on the world, don't waste your precious time courting approval from everyone around you. You can't be all things to all people. Refrain from attempting to be what others want you to be. If you are always trying to please others, you will feel anxious, fearful, and unnatural. There is nothing quite as tough as to live up to others' ideals of what a friend or relative should be. Over the long term, your mental and physical health will suffer.

Success is doing what is right for us and not what our mothers or anyone else wants us to do. Above all, be yourself. "My mother said to me, 'If you become a soldier, you'll be a general; if you become a monk, you'll end up as the pope,' " the great Spanish artist Pablo Picasso once remarked. "Instead, I became a painter and wound up as Picasso."

Again, avoid seeking approval for what you plan to do with your life from everyone you meet — this is BAD, BAD, BAD for business. Keep in mind that your duty is always to yourself. Looking out for number one is important. You must take care of yourself if you want to take care of your family, be generous to your friends, and be of service to your community. Try to please everyone and you may end up pleasing no one.

It is inevitable that you will attract a lot of disapproval as you go through life. This is the price you pay for being alive and for being a unique individual. What others say about you is not only insignificant — but also totally irrelevant.

In the higher order of life, you get to decide what is significant in your world. When you finally get over the need to please everyone, you will experience amazing contentment from being truly yourself. You will wonder why this feeling eluded you for so long in the first place.

43

It's Always Easier to Stay Out of Trouble than to Get Out of Trouble

Think of some of the great difficulties that you have experienced over the years — ones that you invited into your life on some level or another. This applies to financial dilemmas, dysfunctional relationships, speeding tickets, lawsuits, time-wasting arguments, health problems, and family feuds. For good measure, you can add any other predicament that you could have bypassed in some way or form. Wouldn't it have been easier to avoid these situations than trying to get out of them later?

For example, you may have gotten yourself in a financial quagmire. Your bills are coming in faster than you can rip them up, you are so broke you can't afford to go window-shopping, and your major creditors are skulking the bushes looking for you. Obviously, this situation is not simply an out-of-money experience that will dissipate on its own. Because you did not react early, you must now get out of serious financial trouble before the situation becomes even more critical.

The key to staying out of trouble — financial or otherwise — is to control your behavior that attracts trouble. We often invite trouble into our lives when we see something as terribly important, not realizing that, in fact, it is rather insignificant in the higher order of life. Just as telling, we invite trouble into our lives when we see something as trivial, when, in fact, it is important for our well-being and peace of mind.

Clearly, vigilance is the best defense against trouble entering our lives. The person who does not have the presence of mind to identify potentially dangerous outcomes finds it virtually impossible to avoid trouble in the short term and the long term. People who stay out of trouble concentrate on the important matters and ignore the superficial ones. Their response to potential trouble involves strategies on how to avoid the situation totally. They admit to having made mistakes in the past by not taking appropriate action and won't let it happen again.

Clearly, you must recognize and react to the warning signs of trouble if you want to avoid major disruptions to your life. The key word is react. Be proactive and take absolute control of your life. To avoid having to get out of trouble, you must develop strategies to stay out of trouble.

There may be times, for instance, when you are tempted to indulge in a physical confrontation to settle some matter. If you get involved, you are sure to regret it later. Just think of the consequences. You may end up being beaten up. This doesn't sound like something for which you should strive.

The second thing that may happen is you get lucky and beat up your rival. Unless you get some perverted pleasure from beating up people, it doesn't sound like something that will bring you satisfaction. Of course, the third thing that can happen is both you and the other combatant get hurt, in which case, both of you lose.

The way to stay out of trouble — instead of being faced with getting out of trouble — is to choose your life's battles carefully. Indeed, you shouldn't fight a battle if there is nothing to win. Most of the physical confrontations in which people get involved offer no positive benefit to anyone.

When it comes to avoiding physical fights with tough guys, you are welcome to use my strategy. I can proudly report that I won all three of my last fights involving tough guys — by at least half a mile! In other words, I took appropriate action to avoid the dangerous outcomes that usually occur in physical confrontations.

Again, the key to staying out of any sort of trouble is to control the behavior that gets you in trouble. Cool is what you want. Calm, in fact, works even better. In case you still didn't get it, the overall lesson here is that it's always easier to stay out of trouble than to get out of trouble.

44

Don't Take It Personally; They Are Doing It to Everyone Else

Do you take many of the things others say about you or do to you personally? Assuming that you are like most people, I would venture to say that the answer is a resounding yes. As a matter of course we all have a natural tendency to overreact to certain actions of other human beings. Taking things personally is more proof of our selfishness. Each and every one of us who takes things personally believes on some level or another that "this world is all about me."

To be sure, it's all too easy to take things personally. But you must learn how not to take what others think, say, or do personally if happiness is one of your goals. Whether it's getting overlooked for an invitation to an important event, being cut off in traffic, or receiving bad service in a restaurant, don't look at any of these events as an attack or personal slight on you by others. Truth be known, they are doing it to everyone else.

Putting things in the best possible way, think of the person who cuts you off in traffic — along with millions of others on this planet who commit similar acts — as not having have an infinite capacity for decency, particularly regarding manners and consideration for others. In fact, there is something superficially profound about the number of people who can be so inconsiderate. On second thought, maybe not.

After all, the world can be an aloof, self-centered, and disrespectful place. Many people go about their business without much regard for us as individuals. They may not play by our rules because they think their rules are the right ones. For the sake of argument, if for nothing else, we can say these people are just as self-centered in going about their business as we are self-centered in hoping they will pay us more respect.

It follows that it's pointless to get angry with someone who doesn't give you the consideration and respect that you think you deserve. Granted, you want a world in which everyone is as considerate as you. Trust me, this isn't about to happen.

The key to not taking things personally is realizing that nothing that other people do to you is because of you. On the contrary, it is because of themselves — because of their selfishness, in other words. Thus, why get upset about an unreturned phone call from an inconsiderate person who undoubtedly doesn't return calls to anyone else?

You can overcome the frustration of what others think, say, or do by refusing to accept any disrespectful act against you as a personal affront to you. Just remind yourself, "I expect her to behave that way because she is doing it to others. It has nothing to do with me. And even if she is not doing it to others, I don't need her respect and approval." This approach will eliminate any self-inflicted frustration and disappointment that arise when you expect more reasonable behavior.

The next time someone cuts you off in traffic, don't assume that the jerk is rude only to you. Truth be told, he is rude to everybody — even his mother. If his parents in twenty-five years didn't teach him to be considerate to others, how are you going to do it if you happen to catch up with him and yell at him for a minute or two?

Fact is, the jerk who cut you off in traffic has already cut off five other people in the previous ten minutes and will cut off another five in the next ten minutes. Some of the people he has cut off or will cut off are no doubt more accomplished, famous, or successful than you. If the jerk didn't give these accomplished individuals better treatment, why should you expect it?

Let's put things in proper perspective. When we take what others think, say, or do personally, these people haven't offended or hurt us. We have allowed them to do so. To avoid being hurt by people, we must acknowledge that human beings aren't perfect. People possess a large number of negative traits that lead to inconsiderate and disgusting actions. Learn to ignore disrespectful actions knowing very well that these people are doing it to many others. After all, the theory goes, they can't help it. It's their nature to be that way!

45

The More Important It Is, the Less Chance That Anybody Is Going to Do It for You

At some time or another every one of us harbors deeply ingrained hope that someone else will handle the difficult and important events, situations, and tasks that confront us throughout our lives. At the same time we would like the good things in life to come to us as a result of the efforts of others. This is a common phenomenon — it is also insane.

Like it or not — and most human beings don't — there are few significant things that anyone will do for us in this world. Alas, reality continues to intrude into our lives and to make life difficult. You have undoubtedly noticed that the more important it is, the less chance that somebody will do it for you. What's more, if it's extremely important, chances are virtually zero that it will get done by someone else.

Start with the premise that if you can influence someone to do anything important for you, you are setting yourself up for trouble. To avoid having to exert themselves, many aimless people in this world are more than ready to delegate the important aspects of their lives to others. If you get in the habit of relying on someone else, you will run into a serious problem the day that the person isn't around to help you. Besides, individuals who are most astute about helping you achieve something worthwhile know that the best way to help you is to insist that you do it yourself.

Leaving it up to others is inviting frustration and disappointment into your life. There are certain situations when someone may be willing to make certain decisions for you. The problem is that they may not make the right decisions. You must protect your own interests. Plain and simple, when something important needs doing, do it yourself. At least in the event things don't work out, you will have no one but yourself to blame for it.

You must blaze your own trail if you want to arrive at some important destination. As an unknown wise person concluded, "If it is to be, it is up to me." Big-time accomplishments won't just come to you without your making much of an effort. If you think you are being denied your share of the good things in life, you are going to have to do something to get them.

Most of us — above all — are committed to comfort, low risk, and stability. We don't want to work at anything important in life. On the contrary, we want all the important things in life to come without any obstacles, stress, or difficulty. When we are comfortable, we say we are "feeling no pain." Unfortunately, feeling no pain is not synonymous with any of the memorable experiences of accomplishment, satisfaction, and creative fulfillment that come from pursuing and attaining our dreams on our own.

You will attain your goals and your dreams when you are self-sufficient. It's best to take the initiative without expectations of help from anyone else. Friends and relatives have their own goals and dreams to pursue. Most people won't perform important activities for themselves, so what are the odds that they will do something important for you? You can't wait for someone else to get you the good things that this world has to offer. Take matters into your own hands and forget about help from anyone.

It's your life. You — and only you — will make significant things happen. The quality of your life may depend on a number of factors, but 95 percent of it depends on you. Ultimately the quality of your life depends on how much you are willing to put into it. A lot of important things can happen in your life — but only if you make them happen.

46
Belief Is a Disease

Common wisdom has it that there are two certainties in the game of life — death and taxes. Here is another one: Keep believing what you have always believed and the degree of your future well-being and success will pretty much match your present state of well-being and success.

If your life is not working all that well, start with the premise that your beliefs haven't served you all that well. As American humorist Gelett Burgess pointed out, "If in the last few years you haven't discarded a major belief or acquired a new one, check your pulse. You may be dead." The problem with beliefs is they can run — even ruin — your life. In fact, beliefs can become perpetual attachments that hold you in bondage forever.

Beliefs shape the way we feel, think, and act. It is important that you accept that some — perhaps most — of your beliefs may be wrong. Your beliefs may have no relationship to reality. According to psychotherapist Bruce Di Marsico, "A belief is assuming something to be true, to be a fact. A belief is not caused, it is created by choice. A belief about a thing's existence is not the same as its existence." Put another way, gravity is not a belief. It's reality even if you can't see it. But saying that gravity is bad for you is a belief. Beliefs like this one can trip you up in life much more than gravity ever well.

When is the last time that you questioned some of your strongest beliefs? Perhaps it is time that you did. If you take a close look at your life, and find that you are unhappy in general, it's time to get rid of some of your most treasured beliefs. Are you in financial trouble? Are you not as successful as the general population? Are you in a bad marriage? Virtually all the things you have in your life are the direct results of your beliefs.

Much to our detriment, failure to question our beliefs results in our adopting many false ones. It is easy to fall for false beliefs common in society. Good examples are not hard to find. Do you believe reading in the dark or poor light will hurt your eyes? Guess what? There is no evidence to support this. The American Academy of Ophthalmology states: "Reading in dim light can no more harm your eyes than taking a photograph in dim light can harm the camera."

Do you believe that it is dangerous to go swimming right after you eat a large meal? Here again, there is no evidence to support this. Although the Red Cross published a brochure over fifty years ago warning of the danger associated with eating just before swimming, today's Red Cross brochure says it isn't dangerous to swim after eating. No wonder Josh Billings wisely proclaimed, "The trouble with most folks ain't so much their ignorance as knowing so many things that ain't so."

We hang onto beliefs simply because they appear reasonable. Yet a lot of what was reasonable a century or two ago is deemed unreasonable — even insane — today. Throughout history there have been many cases of popular beliefs that later proved to be preposterous. All of humankind, for instance, at one time believed the world was flat. But Christopher Columbus proved otherwise. It follows that a lot of popular beliefs today will be proven totally wrong and ridiculous — even grossly insane — fifty or a hundred years from now.

Modern philosophers and researchers specializing in the study of the human mind claim that we are a long way from understanding how we think. Historian James Harvey Robinson claims, "Most of our so-called reasoning consists in finding arguments for going on believing as we already do." Clearly, our thinking is not as advanced as we would like to believe. No doubt humans living several centuries from now will look at many of our present popular beliefs and ways of reasoning as organized and collective nonsense.

In short, it's okay to have beliefs — but it is not all that wise to hang on to unworkable ones. Unless you constantly challenge your beliefs, you may not be aware that your beliefs have no relationship to reality. Getting stuck in your beliefs can be detrimental to your physical and mental health. Viewed in this way, belief is a disease. Like any health problem, you must eliminate the cause. This means diagnosing your most treasured beliefs and discarding the ones that aren't contributing to a healthy and successful you.

47

Beware of Experts — Particularly Those with the Most Knowledge and Experience

While you are questioning your beliefs, why not question your beliefs about the experts of this world? It's easy to be intimidated by people with a lot more experience and credentials to their names than you have to yours.

What experts are really good at is making a great case for why something won't work. They will convince many people along the way because they are great at putting up brilliant arguments. The problem is that they don't give consideration to why it may work.

A recent experience comes to mind. Shortly after I completed my book *How to Retire Happy, Wild, and Free*, I sent the manuscript to twenty-five major American publishers and ten British publishers. I thought that I would have no problem getting a publisher, but the opposite happened.

Much to my surprise, all twenty-five American and ten British publishers that received my manuscript felt there was no market for retirement books, or if there was, the market was too saturated with too many similar books. I estimated at the time that there were anywhere from one to two hundred retirement books published in English, with the likelihood of many more to come.

Notwithstanding the major publishers' negativism about the potential market for retirement books, I decided to self-publish after Ten Speed Press agreed to distribute the book for me in the United States. I felt that I had likely written the best book in the world on the personal aspects of retirement and that it should eventually prove itself in the marketplace through word of mouth.

It's a good thing, as things turned out, that I refused to be intimidated by what the experts thought about my book. Taking the financial risk paid off big time. *How to Retire Happy, Wild, and Free* has now sold over 77,000 copies and has seven foreign publishers. Just as important, given that I am Canadian, I have experienced an incredible amount of satisfaction from seeing the book do so well in the United States market when so many major American publishers felt it had no potential.

There is a major moral associated with my aforementioned experience — so much for listening to the experts! Since most "experts" don't even come remotely close to knowing whether something innovative will work in their line of business, why not take some chances and disregard what they have to say? In fact, it is wise not to listen to the experts even if they have been in the business for thirty-five years and you are a recent newcomer.

My personal experiences have taught me to be wary of those who try to impress me with their vast knowledge of their industry based on how long they have been there. People who rant and rave that they know more than anyone else — because they have been in a particular field for a number of years — are often the people who don't know all that much. This is likely the reason that they have not moved on to another more rewarding line of work.

I have discovered that often my best bet is to be "unreasonable" and not listen to the "experts." Instead, I find out for myself what can be done and what can't be done in a particular industry. The core of the matter is that individuals who achieve creative success are willing to confront their fears and take risks that others — even the experts — won't. As Robert Heinlein wisely noted, "Always listen to experts. They'll tell you what can't be done and why. Then do it."

Do not — regardless of your limited knowledge — subordinate yourself to experts. "It is, after all, the responsibility of the expert to operate the familiar," observed Henry Kissinger, "and that of the leader to transcend it." No matter how impressive their qualifications, it's foolhardy to allow experts to make important decisions for you. Financial planners, bankers, medical doctors, and real estate agents may know a lot about their field. But what do they know about where your goals, abilities, aspirations, and dreams fit into the larger picture of the universe?

48

Being Reasonable Wins Us the Booby Prize of Life

Martin Luther called reason "the Devil's harlot." Have you ever noticed how reasonable you are — and how many aspects of your life still don't work all that well? Perhaps the more reasonable you become, the more your life is thrown in disarray. This is the kind of thing that happens when your dreams and your actual life situation are not in harmony. You may have to rise to the occasion by throwing reason out the window and becoming more unreasonable.

Society and educational institutions teach us that being reasonable will bring us happiness and success. Granted, being reasonable has its place. The problem, however, is being too reasonable can hinder our creativity and well-being. When we are considering something new and different, we don't have to wait very long before someone tells us that we are being unreasonable. Yet being reasonable wins us the booby prize of life.

Allow me to give one example of the many times that I have benefited from being unreasonable. While working on my Master's in Business Administration, I decided to approach a professor who had given me a much lower grade than I thought I deserved on a midterm paper. What made my going to see the professor unreasonable was that four of my fellow students had already gone to see him about their low marks. The professor became very defensive and refused to give any of them a higher grade.

Reason told me not to waste my time going to see the professor, but my inner, creative voice told me that I still might be able to pull off getting a higher mark. Because I wasn't trained and certified in advanced clinical hypnosis, I had to find some creative way to convince this professor to give me a higher mark. In the end, I took a different approach to the problem than the other students used.

The first thing I did was not make the professor "wrong" by telling him that he graded my paper unfairly. Even though I have a big ego, I made myself wrong instead — desperate times called for desperate measures! I told the professor, "I messed up my last midterm paper which means I won't get a good final mark in this course. This could cost me an assistantship worth $3,000." Then to totally give my problem away to the professor, and at the same time put him in control, I asked, "What would you do if you were in my shoes?"

Much to my surprise — at least to my reasonable mind — my unreasonableness paid off. The professor thought for a moment or two and replied, "I will tell you what. If you make a good mark on your final exam, I will increase your overall mark in the course by one complete grade. Just write a little reminder on your exam that we had this conversation."

As it turned out my final grade in the course ended up much better than I had expected — I got the highest mark possible — and I easily ended up with the $3,000 teaching assistantship. No doubt the other four MBA students who tried to get higher marks never gave much consideration to being unreasonable — indeed, most MBA programs teach students to be extremely reasonable.

Unfortunately, our tendency to be too reasonable leads us to ignore our hunches, inner voices, dreams, and premonitions. We must follow our instincts — instead of reason — if we want to excel in this world. "I believe in instinct, not in reason,' A. C. Benson quipped. "When reason is right, nine times out of ten it is impotent, and when it prevails, nine times out of ten it is wrong."

To add to your aliveness and enjoyment of life, try being a little less reasonable. You don't always need a good reason for everything you do. Telephone someone truly successful to see if he or she will talk to you. Try responding to your inner voice even if it leads you in directions you have never traveled. There will be times when your intellect says no, but your inner voice says yes. Then go with your instinct; it usually knows best.

Being unreasonable is something that you can do on a daily basis. When you encounter either your own voice of judgment, or someone else's, strike a blow against the prevailing reason. You will find life is different. It becomes much more interesting and rewarding because you are living it to the fullest in unreasonable ways.

49

Wise People Learn More from Fools than Fools Learn from Wise People

Not so long ago I received a brochure advertising the annual conference for an international human resources foundation. The cover of the brochure announced, "BE A KNOW-IT-ALL! Here's how." The inside of the brochure promised, "Join our Foundation and see how easy it is to know-it-all." As I read this brochure, I wondered if these professionals — I use the term lightly — had contemplated the advantages of "not knowing it all."

Clearly, no one can ever know everything there is to know in any field — although a lot of delusional know-it-alls think they do. Know-it-alls always think they have the expert answers to any problem. They will muscle you with facts and figures and will arrogantly pronounce their opinion on any issue at any time. Because they feel superior to others, know-it-alls will take it as a personal insult if you do not agree with them on every matter.

No doubt the person with all the answers is a know-it-all. Beyond that, however, he or she is a fool. Put another way, know-it-alls are not as bright as they think they are. Know-it-alls don't pay attention, they don't study or ponder, and they don't listen all that well. Why? Because they think that they already know it all. Sadly, others resist know-it-alls because know-it-alls leave little room for others' opinions and creativity.

Interestingly, the wise people of this world have never claimed that they were even close to knowing it all. Centuries ago the great Roman statesman and writer Cato the Elder pointed out, "Wise men learn more from fools than fools learn from wise men." Indeed, wise people can acquire aphoristic bits of wisdom from people much less talented and educated than they are. Unlike many intellectuals, wise people realize that, irrespective of how much they already know, there is always a whole lot more to learn in life.

The lesson here is that the key to learning new and wonderful things about this world is not ever being a know-it-all. Don't be too proud to learn from people less talented and knowledgeable than you. It's all too easy to dismiss people with less education or intelligence than you when, in fact, they can be a good source of great ideas that you would never generate yourself.

Regardless of how many years of experience you have in your field, and irrespective of how much of an expert you may be in it, you can always learn something new in that field. Sometimes good ideas or information will come from someone you least expect, such as a person who has never had any experience in your field. It may be the resident janitor or a derelict or a Siberian pig farmer. In this regard, John Wooden concluded, "It's what you learn after you know it all that counts."

An effective way to learn a lot about life is not to talk as much as the other person. "You don't learn anything," quipped a wise old professor, "while you're talking." Take the time to really listen actively to others. If you're always too busy yapping because you like the sound of your own voice, you won't learn very much. At the extreme, one-way conversations are conducted by fools although they may themselves think that they are the wise ones.

To learn more, try to emulate the wise people of this world. You should be able to spot the wise people quite easily. Wise people are humble. They are quick to admit that they don't know everything and that practically anyone can teach them something. They listen without preconception or judgment or criticism. They learn from waiters and cab drivers and doormen and peasants.

Socrates, one of the most famous and brilliant philosophers of all time, concluded, "All I know is that I know nothing." Indeed, this may be the greatest wisdom ever — admitting that you are ignorant of a whole lot of things regardless of how much you already know. Above all, remember that wisdom is not a station you arrive at, but a manner of traveling.

50

Be Careful with Your Heroes; Don't Put Any of Them on a Pedestal

"Show me a hero," quipped American writer F. Scott Fitzgerald, "and I will write you a tragedy." The ultimate tragedy, however, is the vast majority of modern hero-worshipers in the Western world who revere false heroes. So much so, that *hero* is one of the most misused words in the English language.

As a matter of course *hero* today is mostly applied to people who do well in sports or in the financial world or in show business and have gotten a lot of publicity. Unfortunately, the modern American hero is somebody whom we adore, respect, worship, or idolize for all the wrong reasons. With this in mind, it's best to be careful with your heroes. Don't put any of them on a pedestal. After all, no one — even a true hero — deserves to be there.

Granted, there is not anything basically wrong when we admire celebrities of sports and popular culture, such as Michael Jordan, Wayne Gretzky, Oprah Winfrey, Jerry Seinfield, David Letterman, Mick Jagger, and Celine Dion. These people have been creative and extremely successful in their own right. Nevertheless, spending too much time watching and talking about celebrities robs us of precious time and energy that could be used in attaining significant accomplishments ourselves.

The core of the matter is that there seems to be a totally unwarranted, yet broadly accepted, belief by the public that modern heroes are larger than life. Given enough time, however, most sports celebrities, movie stars, singers, and politicians end up displaying behavior that astonishes even those who have looked up to them. On the extreme are those pop idols with character flaws so serious that they would make the Devil proud.

Another dark side of modern hero-worshipers is that most live their lives vicariously through their false heroes. If you are living vicariously through a false hero such as a rock star, a baseball player, or a movie star, what does this say about your own character? Shallow, or even deficient, wouldn't you say? Undoubtedly you are telling yourself that you are not good enough yourself as a human being — not proud of your own accomplishments in life, in other words. Living vicariously through gurus, sports celebrities, and movie stars limits you from creating the life that you want.

There is one thing of which you can be certain. A true hero does not live vicariously through someone that he or she admires. So what constitutes a true hero? Hungarian revolutionary leader Lajos Kossuth concluded, "It's the surmounting of difficulties that makes heroes."

Based on this measure, true heroes know how to steer past major obstacles, jump over some more, and blow up even more as they proceed toward their own definition of success. Even so, a true hero is not infallible. He makes mistakes. He sometimes falters. He may even stop accomplishing for a period of time but he never gives up in his quest to make this world a better place to live.

The true heroes are those people who have overcome hardship and made a significant contribution to this world but who are never given any publicity by the media. For example, Father Bob McCahill rides his run-down bicycle through the streets of Bangladesh helping the sick who are too poor to visit a hospital. Individuals such as Father McCahill who work with the street people of this world are doing incredible work. Unfortunately, we seldom, if ever, hear or read about them in the media. These people would make much better role models for youths and adults alike than today's spoiled sports celebrities and movie stars.

All told, even the most accomplished and well-mannered heroes shouldn't be idolized. It's inspiring and constructive and rewarding to use them as role models — but don't live vicariously through them. They have their insecurities and they have their problems.

No human being is worthy of excess esteem from others. Truly self-confident individuals can admire the accomplishments and success of another person, but they don't think anyone is superior to them. They also know that the belief in the superiority of heroes can limit their own power to attain what they want out of life.

51

It Doesn't Cost Much to Be Kind, But It Can Be Very Costly Being Too Kind

Several years ago a woman wrote to Ann Landers asking for advice on how to respond to her mother-in-law, who continually borrowed things and didn't return them. The concerned woman was afraid to say anything because she wanted to stay on good terms with her mother-in-law — who was otherwise in her words "a wonderful person." Ann Landers appropriately gave this advice: "This is going to be a lifelong problem unless you replace the spaghetti in your spine with a backbone."

The moral here is that it doesn't cost much to be kind — but it can be very costly being too kind. Much like the woman who wrote to Ann Landers, many people are so obsessed with being accepted by everyone that they put themselves through emotional turmoil by being too kind. They fear they will hurt the other person's feelings and be rejected by the other person. Sometimes it would be far better, however, if they weren't all that kind and instead gave other people a good tongue-lashing for expecting too much.

As a matter of course we all fall into the trap of being too kind to others at some time or another. Clearly, we must not let the urge to be kind or nice to everyone interfere with our being successful and happy in life. "The disease of niceness cripples more lives than alcoholism," British actor Robin Chandler once remarked. "Nice people are simply afraid to say no, are constantly worrying about what others think of them, constantly adapting their behavior to please — never getting to do what they want to do."

Granted, being flexible and adaptive and accommodating are valuable character traits. Nonetheless, you don't have to listen when a friend or acquaintance runs on for hours about work, family, girlfriends, or rude check-out people. If you are uninterested in hearing more, say so immediately. Otherwise this person will cost you a lot of time and energy that you can utilize elsewhere.

There is nothing wrong with being generous with your time now and then, but constant acts of generosity will lead to certain people expecting this from us forever. As author Harvey Mackay wisely pointed out, "If you want to be a Santa Clause, your sled better be able to pull a trailer." The more you give to certain people, the more they will push their luck.

Being kind to someone by saying yes when you really wanted to say no will cause pain in the long term. If you are too easy going, someone will try to take advantage of you by seeing how much work or how many favors they can extract from you. You don't have to feel obligated to say yes just because the person is your friend. If people are trying to take advantage of your kindness, you have to let them know in no uncertain terms that you don't exist for their convenience.

The ability to say yes or no when you mean it defines your personality and what you stand for. Don't feign agreement with someone in the hope of being in higher standing with that person. You will have wasted time, energy, and money satisfying someone else's desires at the expense of your own happiness and sanity. As a result, you will end up resenting yourself and the other person for having said yes.

In short, discard the notion — forever — that you have to be kind to all people. Being kind to all people can leave you giving so much of yourself to everyone else that you have become nothing yourself. Your willingness to take risks and experience life to the fullest will be severely compromised.

Luckily, there's no obligation — moral, legal, or otherwise — to be kind or generous to everyone. It follows that you should be kind and nice only to individuals who deserve it and when they deserve it.

Keep in mind that not everyone has earned the right to receive you in a nice mood all the time. Be as flexible as your mood allows, but don't bend over backwards to accommodate someone just because that someone is a colleague, friend, or relative. Ultimately, it comes down to this: Do you want to please everyone or do you want to please yourself by experiencing satisfaction and happiness in your life?

52

Being Right at All Costs Is Like Being a Dead Hero — There Is No Payoff

Over the years I received several hundred letters from readers of my international bestseller *The Joy of Not Working*. All of the letters were positive except for about five. One of these negative letters, written not so long ago by an Ottawa man, was extremely critical and slammed me for having penned a book encouraging people to work less and enjoy life more. The letter ended on the note: "You are a traitor. You should be in jail."

In response, I spent about an hour drafting an exceptional rebuttal letter in which I shot holes through everything this man wrote. In my letter I got to be right about my book and made the man who wrote to me dead wrong in every respect. In the end, however, I decided not to mail my rebuttal.

First, I realized how my ego was driving me to be right about my book. Given that I had received hundreds of positive letters from satisfied readers, I really didn't have to prove to anyone that I had written a valuable book. Moreover, it likely wouldn't have made a bit of difference in the way this man from Ottawa thinks. Still more, this character was likely a crackpot who could have taken even greater issue with my letter than he did with the book. He may even have sent me a letter bomb in return. My being right about it wouldn't have done me much good — after all, I didn't want to be right and dead!

Let's be honest. We all get trapped into trying to prove others wrong and ourselves right. The least amount of silver lining in the cloud is that we are driven to be right even though it could cost us severely in terms of friendship, money, satisfaction, happiness, or aliveness. For example, there are many family members who haven't spoken to each other for years due to some rather insignificant argument that occurred years ago. As long as both sides are right about it, no one makes a special effort to reach out and make amends.

No doubt being right gives us validation. There are serious drawbacks, nonetheless. The mind functions in such a way that it always wants to be right. The mind will hang on to ideas, opinions, and beliefs — regardless of how wrong or erroneous they may be. Being right and making others wrong becomes the game. The mind wants to dominate and avoid domination; that's why it spends so much time invalidating others and justifying itself.

Ego plays a big part of our urge to be right. You have to deal with your ego properly if you don't want to get trapped into trying to be right all the time. This isn't about completely getting rid of your ego. This would be the ultimate in being right about it. Putting it another way, trying to get totally rid of one's ego is the biggest ego trip one can adopt. Fact is, you will always have an ego. The key is to be in control of your ego — instead of your ego being in control of you. Otherwise, your mind can go to great extents to rationalize its irrational behavior.

Clearly, making others wrong and yourself right isn't an effective way to raise your self-esteem. If it were, you wouldn't have to keep doing it. Just as telling, making others wrong and yourself right will not gain you much esteem from others. So refrain from being right all the time — particularly if you are afraid of being alone!

To the extent you know that you are right, you shouldn't need to go around proving others wrong. Trying to show how right you are about everything can take up a lot of time and energy. In the same manner that you don't want to agree with everyone you talk to, not everyone has to agree with you. Your position shouldn't be more important than your happiness. The more confident you are about your position, the less energy you have to waste defending it.

The problem with being right all the time is that although you think you have won, you have, in fact, lost — big time! You can end up being right in your mind's perspective, but being right will have cost you a lot, including your overall enjoyment of life. *A Course of Miracles*, a well-known spiritual program, poses this all important question: "Do you prefer that you be right or that you be happy?" All things considered, being right at all costs is like being a dead hero — there is no payoff!

53

The Most Creative Shortcut to Success Is to Reevaluate What Success Means to You

As a rational human being you should always be alert to creative shortcuts to success. Undoubtedly the most serious mistake people make is failing to define success in the most personal way. In this regard the most creative shortcut to success is to reevaluate what success means to you. Ultimately, you will make yourself successful or unsuccessful just by the way you define success.

More of us don't achieve true success because money seems to be the bottom line in our fast-paced, overly materialistic Western society. Advertisers, the media, career consultants, and society in general place a lot of value on money and the things that money can buy, which are in themselves associated with success. Humans strive for a high-paying job so that they can have power, status, SUVs, big houses, exotic vacations, and trendy clothes. These elements of success are supposed to make all of us feel successful, fulfilled, and happy.

There is a problem, however, even if people eventually attain the traditional model of success. When they do, many find that they still don't feel good about themselves. Now they are in serious trouble, because they cannot delude themselves anymore. On second thought, most people still can and actually do delude themselves, but it gets more and more difficult with time.

If you have adopted the traditional model of success, but are not happy and satisfied with the measure of success you have attained so far, it's wise to create your own model. When defining success, we should go beyond the normal parameters and look at what real success is to us individually. No doubt if we asked a million individuals, we would get a million different answers. Every one of us would have our unique version of what we would like to achieve in our lives.

So, what does success look like to you? Besides the general elements of health, happiness, financial independence, job satisfaction, and freedom, what other specific ingredients would you add to your recipe for real success? These should be elements that have not been programmed into you by your parents, advertisers, the media, and society as a whole.

It is useful to take the time to think about and write down the things that really matter to you in order that you can establish your own paradigm of success. With no personal definition of success, you will have no distinct personal goals and career dreams to pursue. Your definition of success may be similar to someone else's, but surely it should not be identical.

Once you have established your success paradigm, it's important to determine which elements are most important for your happiness. Then you must set your priorities accordingly. You must be reasonable in which elements in your success paradigm you want to attain. The extent to how achievable the elements in your success paradigm are will eventually determine how successful you become and how successful you feel.

Here is a warning: For some of us the biggest obstacle to attaining and experiencing real success is expecting too much. Avoid placing equal importance on driving a Ferrari, becoming a renowned entrepreneur, getting a Ph.D. in Comparative Literature, learning twenty languages, becoming friends with both Donald Trump and Richard Branson, having a loving family, writing ten business books, and owning a twenty-four-room mansion as well as a vacation home in Monte Carlo. Anyone who tries to attain this much will likely wind up being a total failure at everything.

Clearly, each and every one of us wants to win at the game called success. If all individuals had their own specific definition of success, they could achieve success a lot easier and experience a lot more of it. Many could also escape the trappings of consumer society that lead to excessive monetary debt and an overly stressed-out lifestyle. What an incredible liberation that can be! As Christopher Morley indicated, "There is only one success — to be able to spend your life in your own way, and not to give others absurd maddening claims upon it."

54

Instead of Criticizing Someone's Success, Why Not Learn Something Valuable from It?

It's interesting and somewhat dismaying how many people will look up to anyone who wins a multimillion-dollar lottery — but will deride anyone who has worked either hard or smart to attain prosperity and real success. Jules Renard put this in proper perspective, however: "Failure is not the only punishment for laziness: there is also the success of others."

American composer Irving Berlin, who led the evolution of the popular song from the early ragtime and jazz eras through the golden age of musicals, wrote more than 800 pop songs. One day Berlin gave a young composer named Cole Porter counseling on how to become more successful in the music business. "Listen kid, take my advice," Berlin warned Porter, "never hate a song that has sold half-a-million copies."

No doubt Cole Porter took Irving Berlin's advice seriously given the huge success that Porter himself achieved as a composer. What Berlin told Porter is great advice for all of us. Instead of criticizing someone's success, why not learn something valuable from it? Whether it's a highly successful song, painting, or computer, we should be admiring and blessing it. Even more important, we should be learning why it is so successful so that we can adapt its positive features into whatever product or service we are ourselves trying to sell to the world.

Anyone who has been a success can teach you a lot. If you resent successful people, chances are you will never be successful yourself. How could you? You would have to become someone whom you resent. Thus, you will always set yourself up, consciously or unconsciously, so that you don't succeed. What's more, you will have a lot of great excuses — but no good reasons — why you have not attained what success means to you.

The core of the matter is that any misfit can criticize and most do. The universe, however, has ingenious ways of keeping pathological critics in their rightful place. It makes them incredibly miserable inside. Moreover, the universe ensures that real success eludes these people for their entire lives. Oh sure, they become successful critics, but that's about all. The last time I checked, there was no Nobel Prize awarded for criticism and I have yet to see a statue made in honor of a critic.

It is a mistake when we make successful people wrong for their achievements. No matter how deserving we are, we can't truly enjoy the things we desperately want until we allow others — even people we dislike — to have the same things just as readily as we would like. Instead of getting you on the road to Success City, criticizing successful people will get you headed full tilt in the opposite direction toward where the misfits of this world hang out. It's called Loserville. So where would you like to hang out? Loserville or Success City?

If you choose Success City as the place you want to be, you must learn not only to avoid criticizing successful people, but also to disregard the negative comments made about you. The more successful you become, the more criticism you will receive. Truly successful people get bashed a lot, mainly by the lazy, jealous, and broke, who apparently have nothing better to do with their time, aside from watching a lot of TV.

Successful people, however, are used to — and spiritually above — the misconceptions, criticism, and untrue statements that negative people utter about anybody and everybody who is successful. Unkind words will even motivate certain already successful people to greater heights.

Above all, keep in mind that avoiding criticism is an unattainable task — even to the most renowned people in this world — because the most degenerate of misfits can easily criticize the greatest of accomplishments ever pulled off by humankind. And, of course, they do. The silver lining is that receiving a lot of criticism from the misfits of this world is a good sign that you are well on your way to success — or that you have already arrived!

55

Your Past Is Always Going to Be the Way It Was — So Stop Trying to Change It!

It should go without saying that it's impossible to alter the past. Yet many people give it their best shot by living in the past. They dwell so much on the past that they never get to truly live the present moment and create a better future for themselves.

Like many people, you may have heard the well-founded clichés, such as "What's done is done," and "You can't turn back the clock," but you still spend too much time in the past. If you presently spend a lot of time thinking about events long gone, it is imperative that you correct your behavior. Regrets over yesterday and fears about tomorrow are the biggest thieves of time and energy. Whenever we spend our time with regrets about yesterday and worries about tomorrow, we miss out on what is happening today.

Perhaps you believe that there is great value in trying to understand the past so that you can figure yourself out — why you do certain things, why you react in certain ways, and why you create drama in your life. There is a slight catch about analyzing the past, however: Most people who spend a lot of time dwelling on the past never do get their lives in order. In fact, the harder the mind struggles with the past, the greater the pain that the mind experiences. You will not free yourself from that pain until you cease to dwell on the past, until you cease deriving your sense of self from past experiences.

If you heavily dwell on the past, it becomes a bottomless pit. You may think that you need a lot of time to understand the past and become free from it. On some level you may even think you can change the past. This is both insane and delusional. The core of the matter is that your past is always going to be the way it was — so stop trying to change it! The only thing that can free you from the past is for you to forget about it.

Granted, there can be a way to make amends for something you have done in the past and this should be a consideration. If not, then chalk the past event up as a learning experience. Give careful thought to what has happened only long enough to figure out what to do differently in the future. Then forget the event and start living the moment for all it is worth. As George Washington pointed out, "We ought not to look back unless it is to derive useful lessons from past errors, and for the purpose of profiting by dear-bought experience."

Clearly, you must give up any hope for a better past. Fortunately, you don't need a better past to have a promising future. Regardless of how lousy of a past you had, it is always possible to start anew. Stop telling yourself that it's too late or you are too old. What is important is what still can be.

Use your energy to focus yourself into the present, instead of wasting it on looking back in time. Most, if not all, thinking about past events that led to your problems robs you of time and energy that can be channeled into solving these problems. Be more optimistic about today and tomorrow and the past will no longer be a burden.

In short, what can be more insane, more futile, than holding on to the past? Whatever has happened before today is irrelevant — provided you declare it so. Your present and future position in life is not fixed or predetermined by what happened prior to today. You can achieve a lot more in your life once you realize that many of the limits imposed by the past are only in your mind. Your future position in life is dependent upon what you do starting today, and what you can make happen tomorrow.

56
All You Can Experience Is the Now, So Why Aren't You There?

If you want to be one of the conscious minority, then you must live in the present and master the moment. Unfortunately, most of us don't live in the "now." We live either the "before," or the "then," in place of the "now."

The notion of living in the now isn't an overly profound idea — yet few of us do it. Not only is it insane to live in the past, it is just as insane to live in the future, thinking about how much better life may be if certain great things happen to you. The key to having great things happen to you in the future is to make the most of the present. As an unknown wise person said, "The future belongs to those who live intensely in the present."

Spiritual teachers tell us that we corrupt the beauty of living by thinking too much about the past and the future. They say happiness is the practice of living in the moment; it's in everything we do. In other words, all you can experience is the now, so why aren't you there?

Believe it or not, THIS IS IT! Now is all you will ever get in life. Such being the case, the degree to which you live in the past or the future determines how many of life's most precious moments you miss in the present.

Contrary to popular belief, the present moment — not the future — holds the key to liberation and enlightenment. But you cannot experience the present moment as long as your mind is occupied with the future or the past. Thus, you should make it a practice to withdraw your attention from the past or the future whenever you do not need to be there — this should be at least 95 percent of your waking hours.

Zen masters emphasize the importance of going through life without carrying around problems and regrets from yesterday and worries about the future. The essence of Zen is to be so intensely present that no problem, no worrying, no suffering, can affect you. The Zen master Rinzai would ask his students, "What at this moment, is lacking?" If you are living in the present, you will realize that nothing is lacking.

Other Zen masters ask the question, "If not now, when?" Enlightened students react to this question by being drawn deeply into the present moment without having to give ego-driven answers. This is because enlightenment — that intensely alive state that is free of burdens and free of problems — cannot happen in the past or the future. It can happen only in the present.

The Zen experience of living in the now is doing something with so much fascination and enjoyment that you lose all sense of time and place. When you are mastering the moment, nothing is important, except what you are doing at that time.

Mastering the moment means experiencing numerous sensations including a feeling of freedom, lack of focus on oneself, and enhanced perception of objects and events. When you learn to master the moment, you will be possessed by energy that carries you away from your normal concerns into a state of optimal satisfaction — enlightenment, in other words.

The importance of living the moment should be as clear to you as a Zen master's moment of truth. If you postpone the chance to live life, it may slip away altogether. The time to start living is now.

In short, at this moment you can't celebrate yesterday; you can't celebrate tomorrow either. So that leaves today as the only day you can ever celebrate. Thus this old adage: "Yesterday is history, tomorrow is a mystery, and today is a gift; that's why it's called the present." It follows that you should accept the past, forget about the future, and surrender to the present moment. Your life will magically start working for you instead of against you.

57

If Your House Is on Fire, Warm Yourself by It

Do you think that getting fired from your present job would be a really bad experience? Your answer is likely "Definitely yes!" Surprisingly, being given the axe — regardless of the stature of your job — can be a good thing. Many years ago I was fired from my position as a project engineer. I was devastated. Yet it turned out to be one of the best things that ever happened to me.

Today whenever friends or acquaintances tell me that they have been let go from their jobs, my response is "Congratulations." I compliment them because I know that for people who want real success in their lives, this is an opportunity for them to go on to something better. A corporation can take away your job and your job title but it can't take away your talent and creativity. By firing you, the corporation may be doing you a great favor inasmuch as you now have an opportunity to fully utilize your creativity and talent in another line of work.

Whether it's getting fired or any other so-called negative occurrence, the event can be a rewarding experience. Anne Morrow Lindbergh claimed, "One must lose one's life in order to find it." Many fired individuals have experienced a new and exciting life by losing their old way of life. They realized that winding up unemployed is a great opportunity to change careers and transform their lives for the better.

The point is that we should remain open to the unforeseen opportunities and gifts that negative events bring with them. I certainly hope that your house, or anyone else's, doesn't burn down. It does not have to be totally tragic, however. "If your house is on fire," a Spanish proverb advises, "warm yourself by it." In the same vein, a Chinese proverb puts things in the best possible way: "My house burnt down and now I can see the moon."

Indeed, there is something positive in most negative events provided that you are prepared to look for it. Having to sit beside a negative person on a long airplane flight is unfortunate. You will have to endure a long, rambling personal assessment of how tough life is. "Why me instead of one of the other 209 other people on this airplane?" you will ask yourself a hundred times during the flight. The least you will get out of this experience, however, is a valuable lesson in how not to be successful in life and how not to make an impression on others.

The key is not to allow yourself to be so overwhelmed by a negative incident that you miss the positive that the incident is offering. A crisis can wake you up and give you the push you need to get something important done. Many events in life can be tough to handle. The payoff is that they toughen you up to handle other difficult events whenever they come along. Make the best of the worst situations and they won't seem so bad after all.

Major problems involving painful incidents or major personal setbacks are often opportunities for creative growth and transformation. Many individuals report that going through a divorce or losing the whole wad in Las Vegas can give the mind a good rattling. Getting fired, as I found out, is the universe's way of telling you that you were in the wrong job in the first place. Major problems are mind-shakers that break old habits of thinking.

Some writers and philosophers say that nothing in life happens by chance. Richard Bach wrote, "Every person, all the events of your life are there because you have drawn them there. What you choose to do with them is up to you." According to people such as Bach, all the things that happen to us are part of a chain of cause and effect. We are responsible for these ups and downs. Our psychic energy attracts the good and the bad.

The good will outweigh the bad over the long term irrespective of what measure you use. The best of times can become the worst of times, but the worst of times can become the best of times. A distasteful event can be good if it adds to your awareness and understanding of the way the world works. Train yourself to see the positive aspects of such incidents and the power of the negative aspects will be substantially reduced. You may feel that you have touched bottom, when, in fact — once you see the positive — you are already headed upward. In the words of motivational speaker Zig Ziglar, "See you at the top."

58
Living Well Is the Best Revenge

Not so long ago an acquaintance of mine was extremely concerned about a nasty rumor that supposedly was all about him. For months he was determined to find out who had started the cheap gossip so he could seek some sort of severe revenge. Months after everyone else had forgotten about the rumor, he kept reminding others about it. Revenge had become his obsession.

Like this acquaintance of mine, many people seem to live for revenge. Sadly, people who become obsessed with getting even for some transgression invite the people who initially hurt them to hurt them even more. In light of their being so hung up on the incident, the bad feelings will probably persist even after any act of revenge.

In the course of everyday living we all are tempted to seek revenge at some time or another. Yet it's best not to get too excited about exacting revenge against someone because the anticipated results appear better than they turn out to be. For instance, if revenge weren't the driving force, most divorces wouldn't require lengthy legal proceedings. Not only does a court proceeding take a lot of money, time, and energy, it swallows up many people's lives. The net result is that even if the plaintiffs or defendants win, they lose.

No matter how bad the transgression, foregoing the chance of revenge is often the best course of action. As Lou Holtz remarked, "You never get ahead of anyone as long as you try to get even with him." It's best to focus your time and energy on something worthwhile. Regardless of how much you feel that you have been treated unfairly, it's important to maintain a proper perspective on the value of revenge. Two wrongs seldom make a right. There won't be any positive payoff — a perverse one, perhaps.

What will hold you back in life is wasting energy on things better forgotten. "To be wronged is nothing," concluded Confucius, "unless you continue to remember it." Whenever you are contemplating some drastic event in retaliation for some transgression, wait at least a few days. You may decide that it's not worth the trouble to seek revenge.

The need for revenge will disappear when you learn how to forgive people who have done you wrong. Paradoxically, when you refuse to forgive, you have not imprisoned the other person — you have imprisoned yourself instead. A Chinese proverb warns, "If you are going to pursue revenge, you better dig two graves." Whatever wrong you have suffered in the past, today is the time to forgive and forget. Not tomorrow or after tomorrow. It's best to consider the case closed. A great burden will have been lifted off your shoulders.

To be sure, all of us get mistreated for no apparent reason. More often than not, it's best to resist the temptation to exchange a bad deed for another bad deed. No doubt the temptation will always be there to get even. Although there is an entire industry based on revenge, including many books written on how to get even with ex-bosses or ex-lovers, we should remember the emptiness that often results from our attempt to get perverted pleasure from extracting revenge.

You won't have to carry a grudge if you adopt and follow this important French proverb: "Living well is the best revenge." Indeed, why not stick to your life's goals and have your significant achievements become your revenge? Along with achievement, there are more subtle ways of getting even. Sacha Guitry quipped, "When a man steals your wife, there is no better revenge than to let him keep her." Oscar Wilde offered the most effective way to get back at neighbors and other troublemakers: "Always forgive your enemies; nothing annoys them so much."

Also remember that fate has a way of paying transgressors back, if not sooner, then later. What goes around has a habit of coming around. People who do you wrong will eventually get what they deserve. Someone else will do something similar, or worse, to them. In most situations there is no need to seek revenge. Just relax and let the gods allocate justice in their own way.

59

You Don't Have to Watch One Minute of TV to Be Happy — and Perhaps You Shouldn't

I hope that you don't belong to the group of unfulfilled individuals who spend most of their time watching TV and the rest of their time contemplating why life is so weird, stale, and boring. If you are a member of this group, however, there is no need to worry. Medication is available to help you deal with this situation. Well, not really. There is good news, nonetheless. When you have had as much as you can take of yourself, you can do something to improve your life.

Start with the premise that you watch way too much TV and you should do something about the problem as soon as possible. Watching a lot of television is a bad choice to make, given that it is not a great way to spend the bulk of your leisure time. "What's wrong with television?" you may vehemently ask in defense of one of your best friends. There is nothing wrong with watching TV half an hour or an hour a day. And there are a lot of reasons that you shouldn't watch more than that.

The biggest problem is that watching a lot of TV is a form of prolonged suicide. If you are going to do nothing but watch television, putting yourself out of your misery may be the best way to deal with yourself. You may as well dig a hole, climb in it, and pull the dirt over yourself.

This is based on my hypothesis that the probability of having a full, relaxed, satisfying, and happy life is inversely proportional to how much television you watch. This hypothesis is backed by scholarly evidence that indicates watching TV is an activity that yields low satisfaction for most human beings. Although many people admit they watch way too much TV, they do so because it is an easy form of entertainment to access. More satisfying activities take more motivation and creativity — requiring effort that many people aren't willing to expend.

The core of the matter is that you don't have to watch one minute of TV to be happy — and perhaps you shouldn't. Granted, watching television, like most activities, is harmless in moderation; many people are not moderate in their viewing, however. Research indicates that today's average American watches four hours of TV each day (or twenty-eight hours a week). That's two months of nonstop TV watching per year. Remember, many active people have a hard time fitting in four hours of TV in a complete spring and summer. What's more, some people don't even own a TV.

Clearly, having a full, relaxed, satisfying, and happy life is about fulfillment and there is nothing very fulfilling about watching two or more hours of television a day while vegetating on the couch. TV is low involvement, not only physically, but mentally as well. A recent survey found that most people admit to being slightly or mildly depressed after watching two or more hours of TV. Highly evolved individuals don't call it an "idiot box" for nothing.

TV steals time that would normally be spent in personal encounters with real human beings, which can add immensely to our happiness. David Campbell and other members of a Harvard research team recently reported that television viewing has a corrosive effect on social and public life. People who adopt TV as their primary form of entertainment are significantly less likely to attend dinner parties, visit friends, entertain at home, go on picnics, give blood, and send greeting cards.

Moreover, these same researchers discovered that chronic TV viewing corresponds with the "jerk-type personality." Being somewhat deficient in character, chronic TV viewers are more likely to give you the finger in traffic than occasional viewers. The researchers did not comment on whether the jerk-type personality is just prone to watching way too much TV or that their jerk-type behavior is actually caused by their TV habit.

Regardless of whether you are actually a jerk or not, creative and constructive use of your time will leave little need to watch TV. In his recent best-selling book *The Four Agreements*, Don Miguel Ruiz reminds us, "Action is about living fully. Inaction is the way we deny life. Inaction is sitting in front of the television every day for years because you are afraid to be alive and to take the risk of expressing what you are."

60

You Are the Biggest Cause of Problems in Your Life

Perhaps this statement will excite indignation from you as do most statements that are true — but that you want to deny: If your life is far from being as satisfying and fulfilling as you would like it to be, you have created this mess in the first place. While facing any predicament in which you find yourself, it's wise to point a finger at yourself first.

Indeed, you are the biggest cause of problems in your life. You have created them — and you have chosen to hang on to them. As some unknown wise person once quipped, "The biggest troublemaker you'll probably ever have to deal with watches you from the mirror every morning."

There shouldn't be any doubt by any one of us that we are the ultimate authors of most of our problems and misfortunes. The consequences we are experiencing are due to our own behavior but many of us are trying to pass the blame onto other forces. Unless we realize that we are creating our problems, we have to keep paying for our actions over and over again.

Never underestimate yourself as a nuisance — or even worse, the major barrier — to getting what you want out of life. Indeed, in your quest for happiness and success, you will have more trouble with yourself than anyone else you encounter on this planet. Some people are able to recognize this; others aren't. Isak Dinesen belongs to the former group. "Of all the idiots I have met in my life, and the Lord knows that they have not been few or little," Dinesen concluded, "I think that I have been the biggest."

Fortunately, overcoming problems and getting what we want out of life is not about circumstances. It's about taking responsibility and overcoming, or changing, our circumstances. If we are willing to suspend our beliefs about our limitations, all of us can be more successful in solving the problems we invite into our lives.

When you stop blaming the rest of the world for your problems, you will gain power and control of your life. Take responsibility for problems in every area of your life. Hold yourself — not the circumstances and people in your life — accountable for your problems. You must be hard on yourself and gentle toward everyone else. Then you have a chance of identifying the true cause of your problems.

You aren't a helpless being subjected to dark and mysterious forces. The next time that you catch yourself complaining about the traffic jam, blame the culprit who put you there — you! Also consider that you are just as responsible for the traffic problem as all the other drivers on the freeway. Incidentally, you have a lot of control over your predicament. Get yourself out of your car the first chance you get and you won't have any traffic problem.

Our actions in life cause reactions in the form of penalties that sometimes tend to be much more than the actions would seem to justify. Some people have difficulty in making a connection between their actions and the reactive penalties because the penalties aren't always immediate. Don't be one of them. In the event you fail to see these connections, you may end up living in misery for a long, long time.

Refrain from creating a big problem out of a mere inconvenience. You will have life's unexpected events create enough real problems for you. Why add to the total? At the same time understand that nothing is as serious as it first appears. What appear as your greatest difficulties today will reveal themselves as your most memorable experiences sometime in the near future.

Paradoxically, problems initiate solutions but the reverse is also true. For every solution applied to a problem, one or more new problems will be created. This means you will always have new problems regardless of how many old ones you solve. Thus, get used to problems.

In fact, you should tap into the world's problems a little more. Without problems, you would not have a means by which to earn a living. Moreover, problems provide you with the wherewithal to get satisfaction and a sense of accomplishment. Now that this is clarified, aren't your problems great?

61

Many of the Things You Want Will Give You More Problems than You Can Ever Imagine

Do you want an exotic sports car? Think it will make you happy? Maybe. Maybe not. A former sports car owner remarked, "The two best days in my life were when I bought my Alfa Romeo and when I sold my Alfa Romeo." This man is not the only person to have wanted a certain dream car, obtained it, and found out that it was the car from hell.

There may be something positive in every negative event but there is usually something negative in every positive event. Best-selling author Richard Bach wrote, "Our disasters have been some of the best things that ever happened to us. And what we swore were blessings have been some of the worst." As Bach implies, the negative in a positive event often turns out to be big enough to make the positive event something that you would rather not have happened to you.

Although this is a hard concept to accept, many of the things you want will give you more problems than you can ever imagine. In other words, be careful about what you wish for, and are working toward, because you may get it. Saint Theresa of Ávila offered some food for thought: "More tears are shed over answered prayers than unanswered ones." Truth be told, many people have found that getting the ideal job, the ideal mate, or some other desire turned out to be the worst thing that could have ever happened to them.

For this reason it is a good idea to give some consideration to the idea that the things you want may not be the things you need for a happy and satisfying life. For instance, if it's a promotion you are hoping for, let the words of Robert Frost be a warning: "By working faithfully eight hours a day you may eventually get to be boss and work twelve hours a day." Indeed, many people have had their dreams become nightmares when they finally got elevated to a job with more responsibility.

A big part of the reason that we are not as happy in life as we would like to be is that solving what appears to be a major problem in our lives often creates many more problems. This phenomenon has many variations. Our biggest concern may be that we are single and would like to be married. Once we solve our problem by hitching up with the ideal mate, some of us eventually end up agreeing with some of the insightful things said about marriage such as "Marriage is lonelier than solitude," "Marriage is death to romance," and "Marriage is grounds for divorce."

Another problem may be our lack of enough clothes. Once it is solved, we don't have enough closet space and can't decide on what to wear. In fact, the more clothes, the harder the decision. No wonder former CBS news journalist Eric Sevareid concluded, "The chief cause of problems is solutions."

Since ancient times, spiritual masters of all traditions have espoused the idea that it's often a blessing that we don't get what we pray for. "When the gods are angry with a man, they give him what he asks for," suggests an old Greek proverb. In the same vein Richard J. Needham stated that "God punishes us mildly by ignoring our prayers and severely by answering them." Still more, the famous poet and sage Rumi wrote, "Some things that don't happen keep disasters from happening."

Preposterous as it may seem, you may want to thank God or the universe that all your wants and needs have not been answered. What appears like it would be Heaven on Earth may seem more like hell on Earth when you actually get it or experience it. Instead of lamenting about your situation in life, give some serious thought to all the severe problems that you have been spared due in part to the fact that you have not got some of the things you dearly wanted.

62
You Can Change the Quality of Your Life Instantaneously

Have you ever considered that your perception of reality could be wrong? If you haven't, this is a pretty good sign that it is. One of the great creations of the human mind is a perception of reality that has absolutely no relationship to it. Thus, you have to be careful with what you perceive as reality. Any misrepresentation of it is a lie. This will cause you all sorts of big problems in life, particularly when you perceive circumstances as much more serious than they really are.

Two people, for instance, can be faced with the same situation. Yet one will view it as a blessing, and the other will view it as a curse. Similarly, why is it that one millionaire can lose his fortune and walk away saying, "Big deal, it's only money, I still have me." — yet another millionaire loses several nights' sleep over a twenty-dollar parking ticket. The difference is in the context in which the two look at situations that reality presents to them.

Change your thoughts and behavior toward problems and the world around you changes. Most negative situations can be transformed instantaneously just by changing the context in which we look at them. The degree to which we are able to change the context of the situation depends on how open-minded we are. By being flexible in our thinking — and challenging our beliefs — we set the stage for fresh perspectives and a healthier attitude about life.

If your life isn't working all that well, perhaps you should give your head a little shake to rattle your mind's perspective. In simple terms, the object is to change the quality of your life instantaneously by changing the context in which you view your circumstances. It isn't the reality or the severity of the problem, but the perceptual choice that determines how you view the seriousness of problems. You may not be able to control certain of your circumstances, but you can control how you react to them.

Don't dwell on the fact that some things didn't work out the way you had hoped. Whatever has happened in the past has to be forgotten and given no significance whatsoever to what you can do with your life in the future. It is always possible to start anew and make a big difference no matter what has previously transpired.

Whatever psychic energy you put into the universe will be immediately reflected back to you. The more positive energy you put into imagining and creating a full, relaxed, satisfying, and happy life, the more it will manifest itself in the real world. This actually works wonders. On a cloudy day, you can create your own sunshine in a split second. The core of the matter is that your thoughts determine your happiness and affect your health. In fact, your thoughts determine the overall quality of your life.

63
The Severity of Your Problems
Is a Matter of Perspective

For some odd reason a large majority of people think that their problems are a lot more serious than they really are. You may be one of them. It is easy to fall into the trap of thinking that practically everyone else out there has a much easier life than you. But as Socrates pointed out, "If all our misfortunes were laid in one common heap whence everyone must take an equal portion, most people would be contented to take their own and depart."

Think that you and your problems are so important? Just keep in mind that the entire world — with one rather irrelevant exception — is composed of 6.5 billion other human beings. Your problems may appear real and important to you — and they are to a certain extent. The severity of your problems is a matter of perspective, however — and that makes most of them insignificant.

Start with the premise that your perception can be unduly deceiving when it comes to your life situation. It's all too easy to internally focus on your problems to such an extent that the wonderful world around you may as well not exist. One reason people have difficulty in handling problems is that they don't stop and ask themselves how serious their problems really are. Most of our perceived dilemmas are just the result of little things that have gone wrong. They are not enough to justify anger or dejection.

As a matter of course all of us blow things out of proportion from time to time. Our minds have a tendency to exaggerate negative events at the expense of our happiness and well-being. Indeed, some individuals react to a television that starts malfunctioning five minutes before the start of a World Series game as being catastrophic. Yet it may do them a lot of good not to watch the game.

The thing that is quite striking is how many past events and situations we have experienced that at the time seemed so critical, but have now faded in importance to the point of being totally irrelevant. Fact is, these events and situations were never important to begin with. The problems over which you are losing sleep today may have the same relevance in the higher order of life

— none, in other words. In a few days you will be wondering why you wasted your time and energy worrying about something so insignificant.

If you think you have big problems — and you are looking for more big problems — you will definitely have a lot of them. Instead of giving yourself a nervous breakdown when a difficult situation arises, put the situation into proper perspective. In the event you find yourself unemployed, sure, it's a problem of sorts. But compared to the situation of a pavement dweller in India, who has to spend twelve hours a day looking for water and food just to survive for another day, your problem of being unemployed in North America is quite a privilege.

Years ago after being fired from my first engineering job — as I was from my last one — an acquaintance commented that adversity builds character. It was hard for me to accept such consolation at the time, but as it turned out, he was absolutely right. Adversity is something you likely won't choose if you can avoid it. But adversity is stimulating in a way because it forces you to use your creativity, particularly when you are really down and out and broke.

Clearly, it's ridiculous to experience self-pity due to ordinary problems. Even the "big" things that go wrong in your life aren't even close to being tragedies. If you want to see really big problems — those that are truly tragic — watch the world news on television for about ten minutes. The point of this isn't to take comfort in other people's tragedies, but to put your problems and situation in proper perspective.

To minimize your troubles, stop and look at the whole picture. Your problems will look rather insignificant and irrelevant to the continued functioning of the universe. What's more, putting your troubles in proper perspective can make most of them look like blessings. In this regard, Richard Bach remarked, "There is no such thing as a problem without a gift for you in its hands. You seek problems because you need their gifts."

64

You Aren't Going to Solve the Problem If You Don't Identify It Properly

"So what's your problem?" This, in fact, is a darn good question. A problem occurs when there is a difference between what "should be" and what "is" — between the ideal and the actual situation. The key to correcting something that is not right in our lives is to try to figure out what is wrong. Put another way, we must identify the problem correctly.

Some time ago, in an attempt to get more seminar bookings, I sent out a brochure to corporate executives. To my dismay, I wasn't getting much response. So I decided my problem was my not having an expensive brochure that would impress executives. Before I spent money on an expensive brochure, however, I decided to kick around my problem. Luckily I remembered something about how identifying a very clearly defined and specific problem is the first critical step to successfully implementing the problem-solving process.

Eureka! I realized that my problem actually was how to get the attention of the executives — whether using a brochure or some other device. Such being the case, I created a puzzle and an accompanying letter that I sent to the executives. Even though the letter was not all that professional, it was extremely effective at getting the recipients' attention — at least one hundred times as effective as mailing the brochure. Fortunately, I had identified the problem properly. Creating a new brochure could have cost me a lot of time and money and produced few, if any, results.

Clearly, to effectively solve a problem, we must first realize and admit that we have one. Most of us can get to this stage. Where a lot of us go wrong is we often dive into solving a problem without correctly identifying it. But, you might think, "If I have a problem, how is it possible that I haven't identified it properly?" Well, many people put up with a problem or an irritation for years because they haven't actually examined its true nature and how it might be solved.

Identifying a problem correctly is not always easy. That explains why British writer G. K. Chesterton once commented, "It isn't that they can't see the solution. It is that they can't see the problem." For example, half of the people in dysfunctional relationships are absolutely convinced that if they could be together with their lover much more, then their relationships would be much better. Guess what the other half believes? The other half is totally convinced that if they could spend more time away from their lovers, then their relationships would be just fine.

Sadly, both halves are misled individuals stuck in a belief system about what will make their relationships work better. The core of the matter is their relationships likely wouldn't improve if either half had their way — whether it's spending less time or more time with their lovers. That is because they haven't identified the problem properly.

The problem is likely a lack of communication. If a couple doesn't truly communicate with each other when they are together, it isn't going to make a bit of difference whether the couple spends more time together or less time together. To say nothing about the fact that the problem could be something other than a communication problem. It could be a self-esteem problem instead. But that's a topic for another book — perhaps even a movie.

Generally speaking, regardless of what the problem is, it must be identified properly. "A problem well-stated," commented American inventor Charles F. Kettering, "is a problem half-solved." By now you should have gotten the message that you aren't going to solve the problem if you don't identify it properly. So don't forget to spend a little time, or even a lot of time, determining the nature of your problem.

What's the use of generating a lot of brilliant solutions when you have not correctly identified the problem? As is to be expected, you won't be even remotely happy with the results if you implement your brilliant solutions. The alternative is to identify the problem straight up front, which means the outcome of your solutions has a fighting chance that it will be a lot more pleasant.

65
No One Can Give You Wiser
Advice than You Can

No doubt you have noticed that it isn't all that difficult to get advice for your problems — regardless of the size or nature. To be sure, most individuals will be more than happy to give you guidance on anything imaginable and declare that it is great advice. A lot of them have likely adopted one of Oscar Wilde's principles: "The only thing to do with good advice," concluded Oscar, "is to pass it on. It is never of any use to oneself."

As a matter of course most people close to you will have opinions on how you should spend your life. Parents will tell you what you should be doing for happiness and fulfillment. So will brothers and sisters, not to mention teachers, friends, advertisers, newspapers, magazines, and television shows.

When I was in my midteens, for instance, my dream was to be either a schoolteacher or an entrepreneur. Unfortunately, I made the mistake of going into engineering because of a school principal's dubious advice. He figured that I would make a great engineer because I was a whiz at math and physics.

Boy, was he ever wrong! I ended up dedicating over ten years of my life to obtaining an electrical engineering degree and working as an engineer in a corporation. What a waste of my life — given that I never did get to understand electricity! What's more, I am organizationally averse, which means I am happiest and most productive working on my own creative projects on a laptop in coffee bars, where I don't have to deal with the hassles of corporate life.

Here's the bottom line: Whether it's deciding on how big of a house to buy, how much money you should save, what career to pursue, or how to raise your children, you should be extremely careful about accepting counseling from other people. This is particularly true when you accept advice from too many people. "He who builds to every man's advice," warns a Danish proverb, "will have a crooked house."

The question that arises is: How good is the advice that you receive from others? Free advice particularly is suspect at best. Artist Anselm Feuerbach may or may not have been too cynical when he said, "If someone gives you so-called good advice, do the opposite; you can be sure it will be the right thing nine out of ten times." When people give you free advice, consider their motives, and what they stand to lose should they give you bad advice. Mark Twain put free advice in proper perspective: "He charged nothing for his preaching and it was worth it too."

In general, you should put more credence in advice for which you have to pay at least some money. The person who charges you for her words of wisdom has a reputation to protect. If follows that giving bad advice could hurt her livelihood. On the other hand, people who give free advice have little to lose in the event that their advice turns out to be bogus.

Some individuals have an uncanny ability to invite themselves into our lives with advice that we haven't even asked for. It's okay for them to suggest that we leave our mates or our jobs. If the decision turns out to be completely wrong for us, however, who suffers? Will they find us another mate or another job? Of course not. They will go merrily along with their own lives while we suffer the consequences of having accepted their so-called words of wisdom.

Advice from other individuals may appear very reasonable to them, and it may appear reasonable to you. Some decisions, nonetheless, are best made intuitively instead of reasonably. Listen to that inner voice when making decisions. Don't become overly logical and practical.

Accepting too much guidance from people can leave the responsibility for your life in the hands of others. You must feel free to do it your own way. Don't allow anyone to make decisions for you, no matter how good they are at making decisions in their own lives.

"Think wrongly, if you please," remarked British writer Doris Lessing, "but in all cases think for yourself." Ask for other people's advice, give it some consideration, and then make your own decisions. Since we are discussing advice, allow me to give you some of my own. My best advice for you is to never accept anyone else's advice — after all, nobody can give you wiser advice than you can.

66

Take Special Care of Yourself
— Because No One Else Will!

In most Western nations today, the plethora of ever-evolving laws can overwhelm us. Luckily, there is still no law that says we can live only to a certain age or at a certain level of health and happiness. Many individuals take advantage of this; they live much longer and healthier and happier than others. Millions of others, unfortunately, allow their health to slide through sheer neglect.

Given that health is an important element of happiness, these neglectful people set themselves up for unhappiness later in life. Although some people with poor physical health, but great mental health, can still experience a good measure of happiness, it doesn't come easily. Staying physically and mentally active is the easiest way to be happy. The degree to which we maintain our mental and physical fitness will largely determine how fulfilling our later years will turn out.

Perhaps you know several people in their seventies and beyond who are in excellent mental and physical condition. They are living life with more vigor and joy than most people in mid-life. They play tennis or hockey, run, walk, hike, dance, communicate, and debate with the same amount of energy that they had in their thirties or forties.

On the other hand, you undoubtedly know many people only in their forties or fifties who appear lazy, tired, and unenthusiastic. For them, getting out of bed in the morning, twisting a bottle cap, or turning on the TV set is a major project. Not only is their physical well-being significantly compromised by mid-life, but their mental well-being is far from what it used to be. They are negative, complain a lot, and never seem to learn anything new. To add to their woes, their spiritual health leaves a lot to be desired.

The $64,000 question is: What measure of physical, mental, and spiritual fitness would you like to have in your retirement years? Undoubtedly, like everyone else, you want to wind up among the active people with an incredible *joie de vivre*. Now the million-dollar question is: What are you doing about it today? This question applies whether you are presently in your late thirties and working at a full-time job or in your sixties and fully retired.

Paradoxically, many working people who say they look forward to an active and healthy retirement are setting themselves up for the opposite. By working too much, many workers are subjecting their bodies to excessive stress that can lead to many ailments, including cancer. Others are also eating too much, watching too much TV, and exercising too little. Still others keep on smoking cigarettes despite all the evidence that smoking dramatically increases the risk of serious health problems such as cancer, heart disease, and emphysema.

It behooves you to do everything within your power to maintain good health now so that you still have it in your later years. In the event that you still have great health, it is a mistake to take it for granted. Great health is often not appreciated until it's lost — sometimes for good. For certain, there are no quick fixes for regaining your health once you lose it.

The Constitution of the World Health Organization defines health as "a state of complete physical, mental, and social well-being, and not merely the absence of disease or infirmity." In the event that you are less healthy than you should be, you should put a lot more time and energy into improving your health than increasing the size of your retirement portfolio. Retiring rich, but unhealthy, won't do you much good. Without good health you can never be truly rich.

Thus, take special care of yourself — because no one else will! You will have to put the time and effort into maintaining your health even when you reach one hundred. More than anyone else, you are responsible for your health. Neither your doctors nor your hospital nor your health insurance policy can do one hundredth as much for your health as you can. It comes back to maintenance and prevention — your three best doctors will always be wholesome food, exercise, and a positive attitude.

67
A Walk or Run in Nature Is the Best
Medicine for Most of Your Ailments

Depending on how you handle and reduce the normal stresses of daily life, you can end up a bright light, a flickering one, or a complete burnout. Often we don't pay enough attention to how daily stress can interfere with our health and contribute to illness. When we find ourselves feeling a little down, it's best to rejuvenate our spirits by reconnecting with Nature.

Some days you may be so stressed that you think you have a nervous breakdown coming on. The battle that rages within can scramble your brain — or even run you completely off your rails. Instead of seeing a psychologist, head for the closest park, seashore, or forest. Fact is, an encounter with Nature is the best medicine for many of your ailments. Walking or running outdoors will do more to relieve your stress, and revitalize you, than prescription drugs, six Miller Lites, two hours of TV, a big meal, or a visit to your therapist.

In fact, you shouldn't wait until you get to that super-stressed-out state. "The trouble with the fast lane," observed John Jensen, "is that you get to the other end in an awful hurry." Start noticing your stress early on before it starts affecting you in any significant way. Relax both your body and your mind by getting closer to Nature.

We keep forgetting about the many benefits Nature has to offer us. The more humans have removed themselves from Nature, the more alienated from the world they have become. If you are an in-tune person, you will find walking through a park or the woods much more satisfying than spending time in a room full of gadgets, trinkets, and other trappings of modern society.

What comes via Nature costs little or nothing. Instead of thinking you have to join a fitness club, get into the habit of using the outdoors as your personal gymnasium. Being outside the house or office is in itself a great remedy for stress. The sounds, smells, and rhythms of Nature compel us to slow down and relax. At least once a month take the opportunity to spend the whole day outdoors in order to get away from your normal surroundings.

One of my favorite T-shirts has a picture of a mountain goat riding a bicycle. Underneath is this good advice: "Have an out-of-car experience. Walk and bike, feel the wind, meet friends, see wildlife, and be part of Nature." Instead of going for a car ride, take a bicycle trip of five miles or more where you will be exposed to the elements — to all the sights, sounds, and smells along the way. You will experience a myriad of things you can never experience traveling the same route in a car.

Researchers give other reasons why you should take advantage of being outside of your apartment or house as much as possible. Studies show that there are twenty to thirty times as many pollutants in the average house as there are outside. For a healthier you, try to spend at least thirty minutes outside each day. Health professionals state that deep breathing exercises are important for optimum health. It follows that outside in the woods, where the air is fresher and cleaner, is the best place to practice deep breathing.

Be a part in Nature's big picture more often. Not only will you feel better, you will value life more. Listen for all of the interesting sounds. Pay attention to the things bright and beautiful. Try stargazing, bird-watching, and sailing. Be adventurous on your walks. Hug twenty different types of trees. Chase wild animals. Get outdoors right now and see how refreshed and relaxed you feel! All told, an encounter with Nature will do wonders for your physical well-being and psychological outlook on life.

68
The Shortcut to Being Truly Fit and Trim
Is Long-Term Rigorous Action

In his later years, the nineteenth-century Italian composer Rossini loved to work in bed. He had become so lazy, according to some rumors, that if he dropped a sheet of music, he would rewrite the whole page rather than get out of bed and pick it up. Undoubtedly, many North Americans today would give Rossini a good run for his money when it comes to lethargy. Even though they would like to be fit and trim, inactivity is their forte.

To be sure, everyone wants to be fit and trim; unfortunately, not very many people want to pay the price. With so many benefits to be reaped from regular exercise, it's a mystery to health professionals why more people aren't physically active. The correlation between healthy people and regular physical exercise is irrefutable, yet less than 10 percent of American adults exercise vigorously at least three times a week.

As *USA TODAY* not so long ago reported, "Despite years of study and millions of dollars spent, despite evidence that physical activity is a key to robust health, long life, and good looks, despite all we know about cholesterol and heart disease and diabetes and obesity, the fact remains — we are a nation of sloths!"

As it turns out, the shortcut to being truly fit and trim is long-term vigorous action. French writer and political theorist Pierre Joseph Proudhon proclaimed, "The chief condition on which, life, health, and vigor depend, is action. It is by action that an organism develops its faculties, increases its energy, and attains the fulfillment of its destiny."

You aren't going to get fit by casually riding a bicycle at five miles an hour or going for a fifteen-minute walk while window-shopping. A Harvard University study found that only vigorous activity sustained for longer periods will get you fit. The study, which linked vigorous exercise to longevity, indicated that playing a standard round of golf couldn't be considered a vigorous workout. Similarly, gardening for half an hour is better than nothing;

this won't get you fit, however. The physical benefit is just that — a little better than nothing!

Here is a warning: Despite its apparent benefits, even brisk walking may be insufficient exercise if you want to live a long life. Regular brisk walking might keep you limber and make you feel a lot better, but it is unlikely to stave off an early death from heart disease, according to a recent research study by Queen's University Belfast. The researchers concluded that regular exercise has profound benefits on health, but that only vigorous exercise — such as jogging, hiking, stair climbing, swimming, playing racquet sports, and heavy digging — seems to make any difference to the risk of premature death from heart disease.

No question — exercising vigorously on a regular basis is not easy. But living in poor physical condition sometime in the future will be much more difficult to contend with than spending an hour or two a day running, walking, cycling, or swimming. Being overweight and unfit will interfere with your ability to enjoy many great pleasures in life. It's tough to enjoy or be good at many leisure activities, such as baseball, tennis, hockey, golf, travel, and sex, when you are overweight.

Don't look around for someone to blame if you have gotten terribly out of shape. Plain and simple, it's your fault for letting yourself go, no matter how many excuses you fabricate. I have designated the weight and fitness level that I am comfortable with and have worked hard to maintain myself at this level for many years. Your duty is to do the same if you want to feel good about yourself.

A fit and trim body elicits the respect of others. More fundamental, no doubt, is that it commands self-respect. If you are overweight and out of shape, weight loss and fitness won't happen overnight. You must invest the time and energy in strenuous exercise. The return on your investment, however, is well worth it. You will be the person with a spring in your step while other people your age will show their age, or look considerably older than they really are.

69
Your Mind Needs a
Good Run Too

Rigorous physical exercise will help keep your body in great shape. Equally important is rigorous mental exercise to keep your mind in great shape. "In a disordered mind, as in a disordered body," observed the great Roman orator Cicero, "soundness of health is impossible." Put another way, your mind, as much as your body, regularly needs a good run, too, if you want it to serve you well.

Research shows that your brain will lose its capability to respond to new challenges and learn new things in the future if you don't give it the mental exercise it needs today. Results of recent studies, such as the extensive research project sponsored by the MacArthur Foundation, indicate that keeping the brain active, engaged, and constantly learning helps to prolong its health and ability to function properly.

Intellectual challenges will not only keep your mind in shape — they, in fact, can help get it in better shape than it's ever been. Over time, our physical fitness will gradually decline, no matter how much effort we put into being fit. But our minds can continue to grow and become gradually more fit with time.

Tony Buzan, author of *The Mind Map Book* and an expert on the human brain, feels that people's memories can actually get better in the years beyond their forties and fifties if they simply take the time to utilize and expand their brains. "The more you learn," declares Buzan, "the sharper your memory becomes over time." This means that there is no reason why you can't master a new language or learn the complete history of the Italian Navy in your sixties or seventies. What it takes is the desire and motivation to make it happen.

If your brain isn't challenged to learn new things for a prolonged period of time, it will lose its ability to discern and assimilate new information. The biggest cause of brain neglect, no doubt, has to be laziness. Spending your entire leisure time watching TV — physical and mental laziness at its best — isn't going to keep your mind in any intellectual and vibrant shape.

It's best to heed the words of someone who should know. Bette Midler may appear on TV, but, in her fifties, the singer-actress maintains a strict TV ban at home, not only for her daughter, but for herself as well. "I won't allow it," she recently told the *TV Guide*. "I made a pact with myself a long time ago. Never watch anything stupider than you. It's helped me a lot."

Several research studies support the conclusion that mental capacity tends to deteriorate when the brain is not exercised over an extended time frame. Activity through challenging activities and intent observation helps to keep the mind in shape. Lawrence Katz, a professor of neurobiology at Duke University, advocates that people do routine activities in novel ways, which use all five senses. Even small things done in novel ways are a big help, especially if you don't have the inclination to learn to play violin or speak a new language.

The key is to be involved in unfamiliar areas and activities. Katz, co-author of *Keep Your Brain Alive*, advises, "The goal is to activate the brain's own biochemical pathways and to bring new pathways online that can help to strengthen or preserve brain circuits." Here are four of Katz's suggested activities: (1) Take a new route to your best friend's house. (2) Choose your clothing based on sense of touch rather than sight. (3) Read a book upside down. (4) If you are right-handed, brush your teeth with your left hand.

There are many other ways to keep your brain in tiptop shape — activities as basic as reading, engaging in active discussions, and playing chess. Exploring new places, learning new things, and meeting new people with fresh perspectives also play an important role in stimulating the mind — as well as helping you experience more joy and satisfaction in retirement.

Nothing keeps your mind in shape as much as learning. Whether it's absorbing new knowledge or acquiring a new skill, learning enhances your mental ability. Being an active learner will not only help you conquer boredom, it will also keep your brain in great shape during your later years. "True enjoyment comes from activity of the mind and exercise of the body," concluded Wilhelm von Humboldt, "the two are ever united."

70
Life Isn't Fair and It Will Continue to Be That Way

Walk into practically any bar or other public place where there is a group of people and what will you hear? Whine, whine, whine — everywhere a whine. If some of these whines are yours, it's time to quit complaining. Nothing is as exhausting as sitting around whining about things — particularly about the unfairness of life. And nothing is as futile. In case you haven't noticed, true success and true happiness don't like whiners.

Haplessly, the vast majority of human beings are stuck on this lower level of consciousness which entails complaining, criticizing, and other modes of negativity about how life isn't fair. Even the media does it. This level is one of low energy and keeps people exactly where they are, never progressing toward higher levels of consciousness, along with true success and enlightenment.

No doubt life isn't fair. Try not to freak out every time someone tells you this. What will set you up for great disillusionment is the belief that there is some connection between what is and what should be. You must accept the fact that there isn't any relationship between the equitable and the actual. Then you must make the best of it.

What you expect and what you are going to get in life are two vastly different things. You may find to your great dismay that the vast majority on this planet do not demand the pleasure of your company even when you accomplish something that immensely benefits all of the human race.

The danger is that a minor setback can send you into a severe tailspin if you believe that life should be fair. Don't be the least bit surprised when your employer passes you over for a promotion, and instead promotes a lazy colleague with ten years less expertise and seniority than you. Fact is, far more serious injustices have happened to better people than you and me. Unfortunately, bad things do happen to good people.

But most of our troubles come from how we interpret, label, and judge the events that shape our lives. Our voices of judgment work to classify things as black and white. We end up spending 95 percent of our time judging people and events as to whether they are bad or good and right or wrong.

The key to making life more enjoyable is to be above all delusions of fairness, rightness, or justice. Be prepared for life's interferences and diversions throwing a monkey wrench into the best of plans and projects. On no account allow any of life's unexpected events to make you angry, bitter, or without hope, however. There is no rational reason why sometimes misfortune strikes and things don't work out. Life can be extremely illogical or unreasonable. It bears no relationship to justice or reason or idealistic notions about how it should be.

It may appear at times that there are no rewards for being good and no gains from suffering misfortune. Nothing is ever lost, however, by putting yourself to the ultimate test to see whether you can be happy under these circumstances. Spiritual masters say everything that happens to us happens for a reason. Our suffering is supposed to have meaning, even when this escapes us at the time. Coming to grips with this spiritual principle will make you less disturbed by unexpected events and more prepared to deal with them.

Although life isn't fair, you have an obligation to do your best anyway. Accept more of what life brings your way and you won't be insulted by reality. We have all felt victimized by other people and affected unfairly by negative events. At the same time we have been blessed with strengths and talents to help us deal with the various difficulties that life likes to throw our way.

Once you accept that life isn't fair, you will be at greater peace with yourself and the world around you. Life will still throw many curve balls your way. But you will be able to hit your share of home runs. The more you can hold up to the trials and tribulations of life, the more home runs you will hit. You may even get a grand slam or two along the way.

71

There Is No One Big Deal in Life That Will Save Your Hide

We all like to believe that there is one fabulous event or one big deal in life that is going to dramatically change our lives. Part of the reason is that in today's world corporate advertisers try to convince us that the good life is just around the corner. Thus, it's easy to be seduced into thinking that something incredible will happen to us, so that from that point on, we can experience perpetual happiness along with problem-free lives.

Because the existence of the one big deal is such a common belief in our society, you may have to regularly remind yourself about this important aspect of reality: No knight in shining armor will come to your rescue. Put another way, there is no one big deal in life that will save your hide.

Here are some variations of the one-big-deal syndrome: If I could only win a five-million-dollar lottery, then I would be happy; if I could only get a new relationship with someone exciting, then I wouldn't be so bored; and if I could get an exciting, high-paying job, then I could start living. People afflicted with the one-big-deal syndrome are looking for an easy way to happiness, where none exists. Waiting for something wonderful to happen is a means of avoiding the effort required to make life work today.

Unfortunately, most people won't accept that there is no such thing as a big deal that will allow them to live in Shangri-la. On the contrary, people believe there is some wonderful event that can take care of all their problems — forever! This is a variation of our belief in Santa Claus when we were children. We felt life was going to be great once Santa brought us all our goodies. Even if we got everything we wanted, our happiness was short-lived. What's more, our lives became progressively more complicated regardless of how many times Santa fulfilled our wants.

If you are like most adults, you still have thoughts such as, "When I obtain this thing, I will be on Easy Street," or "When I am free of this event, then I will be the happiest person on Earth." You are obviously fooling yourself that it will be different now that you are an adult. Wasn't it Benjamin Franklin who remarked, "Who has deceived thee so often as thyself?" So, how much are you fooling yourself? One-big-deal thoughts are hogwash, and deep down you should know this. There is nothing you can ever do or attain that will make your life problem-free.

Think about something that you actually attained in your adult life that previously was the wonderful event that was supposed to make you happy. This could be getting married, buying your dream house, or acquiring a high-paying job. Be honest with yourself. Whatever wonderful events you have experienced, invariably any happiness and satisfaction that you have attained has vanished quite quickly.

Wishing for something incredible to happen is one thing; planning one's life on the basis that it will actually happen is even more serious. Many of us are waiting for that one miracle to happen before we really start living. The miracle never seems to come, and if it does, it won't change things dramatically for the better. Life will pretty well end up the way it always has been.

It is important that you don't put your life on hold until something incredible materializes. You must move ahead toward your long-term goals based on the possibility that you may not ever experience that one big deal. Otherwise, you are shortchanging yourself by limiting your happiness and satisfaction. Breaking free of the need for a miracle allows you to exercise your freedom of mind, and to pursue worthwhile and satisfying goals for yourself today.

Clearly, what will save your hide is the experience of true freedom — from fear and suffering and from an illusionary state of a lack and insufficiency in this world. When you learn how not to want the one big deal, how not to need the one big deal, how not to grasp for the one big deal, and how not to cling to the one big deal, you will have that one big deal in life that saves your hide. Paradoxically, you will have attained that one big deal in life because you don't need it any more.

72

The World Doesn't Owe You or Me or Anyone Else a Comfortable Living

Author Robert DeRopp observed that human beings inhabit a world of delusions, which obscures reality to such an extent that they are living in a world of waking fantasies. The one-big-deal-in-life belief is just one of the many delusional fantasies that many of us hold on to. A more serious ailment than believing in the hide-saving one big deal in life is believing that the world owes us a comfortable living.

The-world-owes-me-a-living ailment is easy to catch. Failure to cure this ailment in its early stages can result in it becoming a chronic disease. People suffering from the world-owes-me-a-living syndrome live a life based on what ought to be. As previously indicated, living a life based mainly on what the world ought to be — instead of the way it is — can have serious implications. In fact, the consequences are usually quite severe. That's why so many North Americans are addicted to gambling, drugs, and alcohol.

The thing that is quite striking is the various justifications that people will give for why the world owes them a means of support. These justifications are all false, however. Fact is, the world doesn't owe you or me or anyone else a comfortable living. These people should pay heed to Mark Twain who said, "Don't go around saying the world owes you a living. The world owes you nothing; it was here first."

Perhaps, like a lot of us, you tend to fall into the trap of believing that someone else will handle the challenging areas of your life, including paying for your way in this world. You may even feel justified in expecting someone else to provide you with a comfortable living. Being no opponent to your comfort and happiness, I will concede that — compared to me — you probably deserve it. Unfortunately, based on this measure, so do at least six billion others on this planet!

Like it or not, no one is liable to provide you and six billion others with a comfortable living. Even if it were possible to attain some of the things you want without any effort, why would you bother? This could not be considered real success. To feel truly successful, you must experience a sense of achievement and feel that you deserve the things you have acquired.

Like it or not — and most individuals don't — a decent living won't come to you until you deserve it. "As you sow, so shall you reap." Clearly, a comfortable living will elude you as long as you are doing what's wrong for you and — needless to say — it will come relatively easy when you are doing what's right for you.

You still have to pay your dues, as should be the case, if you want a decent living. Your deeds, good or bad, will repay you in kind. Paying your dues takes time. First, you must put a lot more into new projects and goals than you get out of them. You will be devoting five to ten times in inputs — money, time, or energy — than what you are getting back in outputs. Later, you will break even by getting back equal to what you are putting in.

There will come a grand time, however, when you are getting back in return ten to twenty times what you are putting in. People will then think how extremely lucky you are to make a comfortable living with relatively little effort. Lean back, relax, enjoy yourself, and care not what other people think.

73

You Can't Always Get What You Want, But You Can Get a Lot More than You Think You Can

As you watch the Porsches, Mercedes, Lexuses, and BMWs cruise Broadway, it's easy to think that you are missing out on the good things that this world has to offer. You may yearn — as I sometimes do when I am not thinking clearly — for a brand-new red Mercedes or silver Porsche convertible. If you want to find out for sure whether owning a new, sleek sports car will make a difference in the joy you get out of life, then you have to do what it takes to get one.

Clearly, you can't get enough money to buy everything in the world. As is to be expected, the rest of us would be pretty hostile. And where would you put it? Like most people, however, you are probably limiting yourself in what you can accomplish and acquire in this world. Although you can't always get what you want, you can get a lot more than you think you can. An expensive sports car is something you can acquire if it's important enough to add to your feeling of success.

You can obtain significant success regardless of how little success you have already. Just thinking you are successful with what others would consider to be little success will put you in the frame of mind to attain much more success. Your perception of being successful with whatever you presently have — money, possessions, accomplishments, and talent — will motivate you to seek other things you would like. With a positive frame of mind, you will achieve these things a lot easier.

A major barrier to our success is our unwillingness to accept that the world just may be willing to give us many more of the things we want — including a dream job at which we can enjoy ourselves and can earn a decent income. More than being afraid of failure, perhaps, we are frightened by the possibility of success.

Oddly enough, some of us don't want to give up negative beliefs that have been a large part of our lives for a long time. The behaviors of criticizing successful people, complaining about our lousy circumstances, and envying talented individuals would have to be sacrificed for a more positive view of the world. We find it easier to remain in a familiar, negative comfort zone than to opt out for a strange, positive one.

Operating closer to our potentials is the key to capitalizing on more of the opportunities that life throws our way. People truly victimized by poor upbringing, misfortune, bad health, poverty, and little formal education have been incredibly successful. Yet people with many good breaks, impressive family backgrounds, proper upbringing, high formal education, plenty of financing, and great health have screwed up their lives beyond belief.

Ultimately, getting much more of what we want is not all that difficult. It's not so much a matter of being exceptional compared to others or of working long and hard hours. Instead, it's a matter of how effectively and efficiently we utilize what we have. This means putting our talents, skills, and available resources to the best possible use.

Although most people are too lazy to creatively put their talents, skills, and resources to better use, there are a lot of us who are not. Being in the latter group will bring you many things you want in life, including satisfaction and happiness. Contrarily, being in the former group will give you high blood pressure, ensure that you remain in a rotten job, and keep you living in that dump in Loser Village. To be sure, emptiness and dejection often catch up with individuals who sit around waiting for the world to smother them with riches, meaning, success, and happiness.

By choosing to be in the former group, you make it a lot easier for those of us who are in the latter group. Less competition is something we don't mind. If you don't want to claim your share of the finer things in life, people in our group of creative achievers will gladly add it to our share. Abraham Lincoln had a few words to say regarding this matter: "Things may come to those who wait, but only the things left by those who hustle."

74

There Is More to Positive Thinking than Thinking Positive Thoughts

According to many motivational speakers, positive thinking is the key to success and happiness and getting what you want in this world. Much can be said for positive thinking; it certainly has more going for itself than negative thinking. No doubt realistic optimism can help you achieve some truly remarkable things. The thing you have to remember, however, is that there is more to positive thinking than thinking positive thoughts.

Some people have been duped into believing that with positive thinking they can "fake it until they make it." There aren't many areas in life where this will work. Several self-improvement websites quote the words of an obscure individual named Adnan Koashoggi: "If you act like you're rich, you'll get rich." This statement is absurd. If you act like you are rich — when you aren't — you will just be a bad actor. You may even wind up in bankruptcy court.

Clearly, pretending that you are something that you aren't — such as being rich and famous — is imaginary craziness. English author Charles Caleb Cotton put the acting part in proper perspective: "It is good to act as if. It is even better to grow to the point where it is no longer an act." It is no longer an act when your optimism is accompanied by know-how, a good sense of reality, and the magical ingredient called "action."

The bad news is that you will encounter many factors beyond your control as you pursue your dreams. The good news, however, is that you have the ability to overcome these factors. We each have our own strengths, weaknesses, and particular challenges in life. This is one of the great things about being alive. We get a particular hand dealt to us, and it's one of the great joys in life to figure out how to best play it.

Ultimately, however, perplexing roadblocks to success and happiness can be overcome only with action. Getting off the couch can magically start making things work out to your advantage and, with time, turn your dream into reality. The moral is to be found in what are some of the most powerful words

Johann Wolfgang von Goethe ever penned: "Whatever you think you can do or believe you can do, begin it. Action has magic, grace, and power in it."

Extraordinary things are accomplished by ordinary people who have extraordinary dreams and take sustained action toward achieving them. In the short term, the results of sustained action may not appear that spectacular; in the long run, they are. The major difference between the ordinary and the extraordinary is the "extra." Invariably, the "extra" is the extra action.

As you pursue your dreams, you will find that creating a life worth living can be difficult at times. "After climbing a great hill," observed Nelson Mandela, "one only finds that there are many more hills to climb." Sorry, there are no seven easy steps to paradise. Indeed, getting the most out of life will take a lot of dedication, commitment, and keeping your word to yourself. This means that the demands of true success will be far too much for most people.

Alas, when the going gets tough, most people disappear. Don't be one of them. You must pay your dues to have a full, relaxed, satisfying, and happy life. This means you have to be totally dedicated to the purpose you have chosen. Anything short of this means that you will probably bail out at the first sign of trouble, regardless of how many books on positive thinking you have read and how many motivational courses you have attended.

To succeed, you must take inspired action! The universe helps those who help themselves. It is in your best long-term interest not to be the person telling everyone something can't be accomplished. Instead, join the successful people already doing it. You must spot opportunities and capitalize on these when you find them. You must also have ambition, determination, and the ability to learn from your mistakes if everything doesn't work out.

In short, positive thinking in itself will not attract what you want. Wishful thoughts require commitment and responsibility. If you want to improve your lifestyle, if you want to have an opportunity for your creativity to make a difference in this world, you have to make it happen. The only motivation you need is the knowledge that millions of people with questionable intelligence and talent win at the game of success. If they can do it, so can you — with action!

75

What Will Keep You from Getting What You Want Is Not Knowing What You Truly Want

This question is simple but has profound implications — it isn't an easy one to answer. The question is: What do you really want? Clearly, knowing what we truly want is a prerequisite to leading a full, relaxed, satisfying, and happy life. But do we really know what we want? According to American labor and political leader Eugene V. Debs, "The American people can have anything they want; the trouble is they don't know what they want."

Indeed, most of us are in a daze. We haven't even realized what it is exactly that we want. Moreover, we haven't realized the power that we have in creating some of the things we desire out of life. The core of the matter is that we have to stop lying to ourselves about what we truly want if we want to eventually get what we truly want. "Unhappiness is not knowing what we want," stated humorist Don Herold, "and killing ourselves to get it."

Most Americans are, in fact, killing themselves pursuing what they don't truly want. Probably the hardest thing about living a satisfying and prosperous lifestyle is to be true to your own dreams and refrain from going along with the masses. Even at the best of times, chasing after what everyone else is chasing is a zero-results game. To be like everyone else is to lose your true self.

So, what do you want? Sure, you want to look better, feel better, work less, make huge amounts of money, have more leisure time, and become more important than everyone else. Me too! See, we do have something in common. But doesn't practically every North American desire these things? The problem with these wants is they are too general.

"Men go fishing all their lives," observed Henry David Thoreau, "without knowing that it is not fish they are after." So, perhaps you are working hard for a lot of material possessions and you don't really want them. If it is great friendship that you would like, you are wasting your life away working overtime to buy things you don't need or really even want.

Getting to know what you truly want is not as easy as it seems. You just can't say, "I want to be happy," or "I want to be famous." You have to be more specific. Where do you want to be five years from now? New York, Paris, Amsterdam, or Rhinelander, Wisconsin? What would you like to be doing for a living five years from now? Sailing, acting, singing, teaching, or writing?

We must stop to clearly define what we want in a way that shows our wants are unique. The key to a satisfying life is taking the time — this may take anywhere from an hour to several days or weeks — to determine what you truly want. Focus brings power.

The clearer you are about what you want, the easier it is to attract it into your world. It helps to write down everything that is important to you, anything from satisfying employment, to a comfortable place in which to live, to an intimate relationship. Now what do you really want in terms of making a difference in this world?

When you have determined what you want, you must declare it to the rest of the world. According to many modern-day teachers such as Jack Canfield, who have achieved extraordinary health, wealth, and success themselves, when you declare that you want something and are actually working toward getting it, you send a signal to spiritual powers in the universe to move that something toward you and you toward it.

So again, what do you want? What sort of a dream job would you like to work at? What would make you smile by just thinking about it? What would you attempt if failure were no longer possible? You can drift along from day to day with no particular goal in mind. You will achieve much more, however, and enjoy it more, if you have a definite idea of what you want, and how you are going to get it.

In short, you must set some actual targets and not just vague descriptions of what you would like to achieve. Again, what will keep you from getting what you want is not knowing what you truly want. Or as legendary motivational speaker Zig Ziglar put it, "It's just as difficult to reach a destination you don't have as it is to come back from a place you have never been."

76

You Aren't Going to Get Much of What You Want Unless You Ask for It

Let's say that you have determined the true wants that will definitely contribute to your happiness and well-being. The core of the matter is that most of these desires won't be fulfilled on their own. Whether your wants entail career, romantic, personal, or creative changes in your life, you are going to need the help of certain people to attain them.

One of life's fundamental truths is "Ask and you shall receive." Put another way, the universe responds to individuals who ask others for the things that they truly want. Most people in this world, however, end up never achieving or receiving what they imagine in their dreams simply because they never ask.

Clearly, waiting for someone to give you whatever you long for isn't the way to get it. Don't allow the thought "It's rude to ask" deter you from asking for what you want. Although many people abide by this social conditioning, most — if not all — are still waiting for the break, invitation, salary increase, radio interview, date, or forgiveness that they desire.

In any kind of human relationship, we have a habit of assuming that others are aware of our hearts' desires. We figure that we don't have to express what we want. If they don't do or give us what we desire, we feel slighted and think, "How could you do that to me? You should know what I want." This is a common response that doesn't bring results. Fact is, when you take control by asking for what you want, you can have a much more satisfying life.

First, you have to ask yourself for permission and then you have to give yourself permission to get what you want. You shouldn't have any guilt feelings about possibly acquiring what you desire when you ask someone for it. You have to believe that you deserve it. Do not ask for it apologetically; otherwise, the person will detect that you don't think that you deserve it. Ask in such a way that the person is happy to give it to you.

Before you ask someone for something that will make you happier, however, ensure that the person will be able to provide it to you. Some people are very qualified and will be pleased to help. Others just aren't capable of delivering. Don't waste your time asking someone who is incapable of giving it to you.

You have to ask the person who has the power, position, money, energy, time, charm, or expertise to give it to you. Individuals who are capable of providing what you want may be more than willing to help you get it. Just like you, they want to help others and feel good about it. They can't read your mind, however.

Just as important, keep in mind that you must always give something to get something in return. "You can get everything in life you want," according to Zig Ziglar, "if you will just help enough other people get what they want." You must convey how the individual will benefit and win when he or she provides you with what you desire. Surprisingly, when you truly need certain things in life, certain people will provide you with them.

People won't know for certain what is on your mind unless you truly communicate your thoughts. Whenever you yearn for something, state what it is clearly and loudly. Leave no doubt in anyone's mind that you want it. Keeping them guessing all the time will have them continually jumping to wrong conclusions about where you are coming from.

You shouldn't expect to always be given what you want after just one request. Sometimes you will have to ask and ask again several times. Some people won't get it that you are serious until you have asked ten or twenty times. When one way of asking doesn't work, you may have to ask in a different way. Most tasks can be accomplished in several ways — and there is more than one way to ask for what you want. When you find a way to ask that works, keep on using it.

One of life's joys is to have developed the ability to ask for what you want in such a way that many people are delighted to give it to you. The more that you ask for things, the better you will be at it. And the more you ask, the more you will receive provided you truly want it — and, of course, deserve it.

77

Getting Rid of Your Desire for Something Is As Good As Possessing It

Writer Margaret Titzel posed this important question: "Why are we surprised when fig trees bear figs?" One revealing answer, alas, is that we are expecting something completely different — such as gems or diamonds or cold hard cash instead of figs. Fact is, reality has a habit of sobering us when our expectations are excessive.

All things considered, our expectations cause us the most disappointment in our lives. Ancient Buddhist teachings tell us that unfulfilled desires and expectations create unhappiness. It follows that the more expectations you have, the more unhappiness you are likely to experience. Even when something good comes your way, you will not feel grateful once you get it.

For this reason it's wise to review your expectations regularly. The great things that you are expecting may not be expecting you. Whenever your expectations are excessive, what you want and what you are going to get in life will end up being two vastly different things.

There is nothing wrong with wanting new things in your life, but desperately wanting them is the perfect way to set yourself up for much disappointment and dejection. If you regularly hope for something that is unlikely to happen, such as winning a one-million-dollar lottery, you will constantly experience unhappiness in your life. This is a textbook example of delusional thought being used to mask reality and replace it with irresponsible fantasy.

Contrary to popular modern-day beliefs, fewer expectations about what life has to offer can enhance your life immeasurably. This may seem like a far-out idea and it is. But it works. Zen philosophy teaches us that the less we need in material and physical comforts, the freer we become. This means that getting rid of your desire for something is as good as possessing it — and often less trouble!

Fulfillment is always there if you want it. It is not as important to increase your acquisitions as it is to scale down your wants. "Blessed be he who expects nothing," said Jonathan Swift, "for he shall never be disappointed." The question really has to do with what we need versus what we want. We must know where to draw the line between "must-haves" and "would-like-to-haves." Most of the apparent must-haves — in reality, things that we don't need at all — demand way too much of our time, energy, and money.

Looking at the big picture, most things in this world don't really matter. It's a big mistake to pursue them at the expense of the few things that do matter. To hold your expectations in check, you must understand that you have few real needs. You are a creation mainly of wants and only of a few needs. Indeed, every necessity has always been provided for you in your life so far. Plain and simple, if they weren't — you would be dead!

Your mind may be your greatest asset, but remember that it can play tricks on you as well. The most common trick it plays is making you believe that you need all the things that you would like. If you allow it to keep playing that nasty trick, it can cost you your health, your individuality, your self-esteem, and your sanity. Above all, it can cost you a full, relaxed, happy, and satisfying life.

Life will always seem like a major rip-off when you expect to get everything you want. You will continue dreaming the delusional dream while waiting for happiness to find you. It ain't going to happen. This world is not all about you. There is a much bigger picture than your expectations. As Bertrand Russell so wisely pointed out, "To be without some of the things you want is an indispensable part of happiness."

If you do not hold your wants in check, you will never be happy. The worst mistake you can make is expecting to have it all, which is what advertisers want you to believe is possible. This is the bottom line about having it all: If you expect to have it all, you will always feel like you have nothing. If you learn to be happy with nothing, however, you will always feel like you have it all.

78

Want What You Have and You Will Always Get What You Want

Economists say that all of us have wants that are insatiable. If this is the case, happiness should be attainable by no one. Yet there are people in this world who are much happier and much more satisfied than others. Obviously they have placed their wants in check or already gotten most of the things that they want out of life.

Ultimately, the best way to get what you want is to want what you have. The less we want, the freer and happier we become. In this regard, an unknown wise person once remarked, "Success is getting what you want; happiness is wanting what you get." The Buddhists express the same wisdom with this proverb: "Want what you have and you will always get what you want."

Of course, over the ages many wise spiritual people of this world have advised that we be grateful for what we have. Now there is scientific evidence that gratitude enhances our well-being. Not so long ago researchers at the Universities of California and Miami reported that people who consciously remind themselves every day of the things they are grateful for show marked improvements in mental health and some aspects of physical health.

The results appear to be equally true for healthy college students and people with incurable diseases, according to the researchers who published their findings in the *Journal of Personality and Social Psychology*. Compared with groups of subjects who counted hassles, such as hard-to-find parking spots, grateful people felt better about their lives and more optimistic. In other words, they were happier.

Many people get a great deal of enjoyment out of life having very little and many people get very little enjoyment out of life having a lot. Your happiness will be determined, not by how much you have, but by how much you enjoy what you have. It is folly to look at what others have that you don't have, and to think yourself poor. Instead, look at the things that you have which many others don't have, and think yourself rich.

Moreover, ten times as many good things happen to you as bad things. Thus, it behooves you to spend ten times as much time ranting and raving about the wonder of life as you do complaining about it.

To become aware that you have a lot of great things in your life, pay attention to the small things instead of the big ones. "Most of us miss out on life's big prizes. The Pulitzer. The Nobel. Oscars. Tonys. Emmys," stated some unknown wise person. "But we're all eligible for life's small pleasures. A pat on the back. A kiss behind the ear. A four-pound bass. A full moon. An empty parking space. A crackling fire. A great meal. A glorious sunset. Hot soup. Cold beer. Don't fret about copping life's grand awards. Enjoy its tiny delights."

Feeling grateful for what you have in life is one of the most powerful ways to experience happiness. Express gratitude for the good things in your life and you will transform dejection into joy. Feel thankful for your health, your home, your friends, your parents — even this book if you really want to stretch this concept to the limit. Regardless of what you feel grateful for, you will realize that you are living in enormous abundance that will result in your feeling happy about your privileged position in life.

Showing gratitude for what you have — to God or otherwise — should be a daily ritual. The more gratitude you express for the things you already have, the less you will need or want. Develop a new appreciation for the things you take for granted, such as the fresh smell of coffee, a gentle wind blowing in your face, and the purring of your cat. And never tire of watching a sunset or smelling the roses. Again, want what you have and you will always get what you want.

79

You Are Already a Millionaire — Your Creativity Makes It So

In my view, Mark Twain expressed a great deal of wisdom with these words: "Thousands of geniuses live and die undiscovered — either by themselves or by others." The fact that so many people haven't discovered they are geniuses is a major reason why they toil away at jobs they hate. As is to be expected, most corporations aren't about to help their employees realize they are geniuses for fear of losing them.

By geniuses, I refer to individuals with the potential to make a difference in this world if they ever get around to developing and using their creativity. Unfortunately, most people have allowed organizations, educational institutions, and society to suppress their creativity for so long that they don't realize how creative they can be. Truth be told, most people can be more creative and, in turn, more successful.

In this regard, there are two principles for creative success — one general and one specific. The general principle is that virtually everyone has the ability to be more creative and accomplish extraordinary things in this world. The specific principle is that almost everyone has volunteered to be exempt from the general principle. Put another way, few people spend time, effort, or thought cultivating their creative ability, which is an essential element for achieving real success in life.

The majority of adults don't get halfway to reaching their full creative potential due to their self-imposed limitations. Sadly, many people have suppressed both their desire and their ability to be creative for so long that they think they are naturally uncreative. You may be one of them.

How many times have you said to yourself or others, "If I only had the creative ability to pull that off?" All told, each one of us has greater inventiveness than we exhibit in ordinary life, but most of us are unaware of it, or refrain from using it. Again, there is no heavier burden than great potential that we are squandering. To deny our creativity is to lie to the world and, worse, to lie to ourselves.

Creative thinking, if diligently practiced, allows each and every one of us to accomplish feats that appear to be unattainable miracles to those who don't practice it. Creativity combined with action is a simple, easy, and surefire way to achieve health, wealth, and happiness in our lives; it is also an invaluable tool to help us experience harmony in this fast-moving and constantly changing world in which we live.

If you are serious about attaining true success in this rapidly changing world, start with the premise that from both a financial and a personal point of view, your most valuable asset is not your job, your house, or your bank account. Plain and simple, it's your creative ability. Your creative mind has great value because it can solve problems.

All employers have problems that they pay employees to solve. In the same vein, individuals have various problems, such as needing something to entertain them, that they pay others to solve. The value you place on your creative mind should be at least one million dollars because you can use it to generate many times this amount over your lifetime. This makes creativity the poor person's wealth. Indeed, when you list the monetary value of your personal assets, the grand total should make you a millionaire simply by including the value of your creative ability.

You, too, can joyfully earn a decent living if you develop your creative side and in doing so provide an imaginative product or service that people want. In fact, it's harder to suppress your creativity than to use it. Everyone has the deep-seated desire to produce something innovative. In everyone there is a creative person wanting to break out and make a difference in this world.

All things considered, your creativity is your biggest asset. Put another way, you are already a millionaire — your creativity makes it so! You must recognize the latent genius within and stay in the habit of being innovative if you want to attain true success in your life. To maximize the use of your creative mind is to maximize the career and financial aspects of your life.

80

If Patience Is Just the Art of Concealing Your Impatience, You Better Be Very Good at It

It has been said that patience is in the eyes of the beholder. One beholder went so far as to define patience as "the art of concealing your impatience." If this is the case, then you had better be very good at concealing your impatience. In other words, you had better have a lot of patience regardless of how you define it. Fact is, patience will determine whether you fail or succeed in most areas of your life.

Patience is described as a virtue in many religions and spiritual practices. Yet this virtue is found in few people today. If patience isn't one of your natural virtues, it is imperative that you develop it on your own — but don't attempt this with breathless haste! Perhaps you admit you're not as patient as you would like to be. Not to worry, just learn to slow down bit by bit, for patience comes to those who learn to take a more relaxed approach to life.

Being patient doesn't mean sitting around waiting for great things to happen to us, however. Instead, patience is the ability to experience waiting and delay without becoming irritated or upset, and to persevere effortlessly when faced with difficulties, while working toward the attainment of our own special definition of success. As the old adage goes, Rome was not built in a day. Above all, patience is the ability to wait — without quitting — for the fruition of our efforts.

Clearly, time is required to achieve or acquire anything worthwhile. It follows that those who lack patience will fail to accomplish much. Too many people in today's American society expect instant gratification in all aspects of their lives. They want — no later than today, of course — a new car, an exciting career, a high income, a mansion in a prestigious neighborhood, a big-screen TV, expensive trinkets, and a happy marriage with well-behaved children. In fact, for some of these impatient souls, instant gratification takes too long.

Putting things in the best possible way, impatient people seldom arrive where they are going. If they do, it is either too early or too late. The more they push, the less they accomplish. To them life is a race against time. This is another sign of success-seekers unclear on the concept of what it takes to achieve true success. They haven't learned that there are situations where it is best to ease off the accelerator and let fate take its course. "Wisely and slow; they stumble that run fast," wrote William Shakespeare.

Keep in mind that impatience can cause all sorts of problems in your life — even the loss of it! Every year over 45,000 people are killed in automobile accidents in the U.S., many due to some driver's unwillingness to wait. Whenever you find yourself in a rush, ask yourself, "What's your hurry?" Then, tell yourself, "Slow down and live!" The extra twenty or thirty seconds it takes to cross that street with your car may add twenty or thirty years to your life, or someone else's.

In the same vein, you must apply discipline to your thoughts when you become anxious over the outcome of a goal. It is impossible to force your preferred speed on the rest of the world. In many situations, you have to accept the natural flow of events. Trying to speed them up is asking for trouble. "There is a time to let things happen," advised Hugh Prather, "and a time to make things happen." In some cases, going too fast can be more detrimental than going too slow. What seems urgent seldom is.

The road to success is paved with lots of ruts and detours. Don't expect to set new speed records on your way there. Impatience can be costly. Your greatest mistakes can be a result of impatience and going too fast. People in a mad rush may appear to have the upper hand today. You will be way ahead of them in the future, however, if you are willing to be patient and tone down your ardor for the chase.

In short, develop the art of patience if you always feel in a rush. Impatience leads to anxiety, worry, fear, disillusionment, and constant failure. Patience, on the other hand, leads to confidence, tolerance, and a healthy outlook on life, which eventually leads to true success that few in this world ever attain. True success, by the way, means having a full, relaxed, satisfying, and happy life.

81
Opportunity Knocks Often — How Often Are You Home?

There are many opportunities around you to prove that you were put on Earth to make a big difference. If you want to do something that makes the world sit up and take notice, however, you must make the most of these opportunities, which can pop up in the most unusual places and at the most unexpected of times.

You know very well what being the first to "detect" an opportunity could mean to your bank account. If you were first to start a website selling an e-book on how to make money on the Internet, which ended up earning you $25,000 a month, would you still be in your nine-to-five job? Of course not, because there would be no point to it!

Whether it's an Internet opportunity you are looking for, or a solution to a problem, don't underestimate the power of your creative mind. Think! Think! Think! Think! Think! And when you believe you have thought enough, think some more. As Winston Churchill said, "Never, never, never, never, never give up." The blockbuster million-dollar idea will always be percolating somewhere in your brain if you really want it.

Many people say there is no opportunity to make it in today's world. That's total nonsense. It's an excuse used by people who don't want to pay the price, or just want to go on in their rut in life. "The only place opportunity cannot be found is in a closed-minded person" is the way Bo Bennett put it. No doubt it's much easier to sit around and talk about the lack of opportunities than to spot some and do something with them. The time that many people spend complaining about the lack of opportunities is the same time that others are utilizing to capitalize on ones they have spotted.

You need not travel far and wide to discover opportunities. The best opportunities will always be found in your own backyard and not halfway around the world in someone else's backyard. You have to look for them, nonetheless. As Ralph Waldo Emerson so rightfully pointed out, "God hides things by putting them near you."

Perhaps you are like many people who have better than 20-20 vision — but even so are blind to all the opportunities around them. Occasionally you must look for what's initially invisible to your intellect, but completely obvious to your intuition. You may even have to close your eyes to see.

Another key to capitalizing on opportunities is to be more attentive to what successful people have to say about all the opportunities around you. Anything important — which takes only one minute to point out — will exceed most people's attention span by at least forty-five seconds. Learn to pay attention for two minutes at a time, and you will have more opportunities than you know what to do with.

In fact, there are more opportunities today than there ever were. There are a few big opportunities and there are countless small ones. It is a mistake to ignore an opportunity just because it appears too small. Truth be known, small opportunities provide the greatest potential. They are rarely recognized as really big things about to happen.

Opportunity knocks a lot more often than most people care to admit! Most people are oblivious to opportunities. If they aren't, they don't take advantage of them. Thomas Edison once observed, "Opportunity is missed by most people because it is dressed in overalls and looks like work." In other words, if you want the door of opportunity to open, you have to do your part to open the door. With opportunity comes responsibility.

If you really look, there are a hundred interesting and exciting opportunities around you at this moment. And the future will continue to bring new ones. "When one door of opportunity closes," observed Helen Keller, "another opens. Often we look so long at the closed door that we do not see the one which has been opened for us." Forget about lost opportunities and focus on those around you at this time. Remember that opportunity knocks often! The question is: How often are you home?

82

To Double Your Success Rate, Just Double Your Failure Rate

Regardless of the route you take to success and happiness, you will always have to overcome barriers and adversity. What's more, you will have to experience failure. But failure, put in proper perspective, can have its positive aspects.

Anything worthwhile requires risk and in virtually all arenas of life risk is directly proportionate to reward. Generally speaking, the higher the risk, the higher the reward. Whether you want conventional success or real success as you define it, you need to be willing to take those risks. One of the greatest risks is failure.

Without exception, there is no such thing as success without failure. Moreover, whatever you attempt, you aren't going to do it perfectly, even if you do succeed to a large extent. Strangely enough, planning for lots of obstacles and failure can add to your chances of success.

Failure, as it turns out, turns losers into winners. Failure can be the best education you get in life. What all the achievers of this world have is a great attitude toward failure. If you want to be an achiever, you must be willing to lose a few battles in order to win the war. "A [real] failure is a man who has blundered," stated Elbert Hubbard, "but is not able to cash in on the experience." As difficult as it is to do, we must welcome failure if we want to achieve any measure of success.

Truth be known, all truly successful people are creative and take calculated risks, expecting that they will experience a good measure of failure. Indeed, the journey to success will always require a lot of failure, which, contrary to public belief, is good for us. "We live in an age of publicity and hype. There's something about success that dehumanizes you," claims award-winning film producer Norman Jewison, "whereas failure reminds you of who you really are."

It has been my experience that the key to success is to fail more than the average person is willing to endure. If at first you don't succeed, you are about average. And no matter what you fail at, there will always be someone who knew you would. Just don't let failure go to your head like most people do.

You will likely recognize this pattern: Failure. Failure. Failure. Failure. Success! Failure. Failure. Failure. Failure. Success! The point is that we normally experience a lot of failure before we attain success. Indeed, the road to success is paved with a lot of failure, and not much else. Thus, to double your success rate, just double your failure rate. Life is remarkably easy sometimes, isn't it?

There will be days when nothing goes right. But not all is lost. Quite the contrary. You will learn more from one day of big problems and difficulties than you will learn from a month of total pleasure and comfort. Congratulate yourself for the smallest of successes — and for the biggest of failures. In Texas when they lose, they lose big — and they brag about it! To brag about your failures is to take responsibility for them.

To be sure, the greater the success you become, the more blunders you will have to your name. One failure gets you started on the road to success; a hundred get you there. Above all, failure must be taken in stride and with humor. After having lost over $40,000 on one of his patents, Mark Twain declared, "I gave it away to a man whom I had long detested and whose family I desired to ruin."

Don't be dismayed whenever some important things don't work out. From a spiritual point of view, failure is the universe's way of ensuring that too much success doesn't happen all at once. Failure is also the universe's way of ensuring that you enjoy your success once you attain it. In short, a life without failure won't get you anywhere worth going — a life with a lot of failure will, however.

83

Compromising Your Integrity for Money, Power, or Fame Will Come Back to Haunt You Big Time

Today it's impossible to find something illegal, immoral, unethical, or disgusting that people won't do for money, power, or fame. For instance, people will lie to spouses, steal from decent employers, commit burglary, injure innocent people, kidnap helpless children, sell their own children, have sex with strangers, and kill relatives for some extra cash.

Others will even consider selling their souls with the expectation of receiving a princely sum for them. Alas, they don't give this enough thought. Apparently many others are looking for an easier go-around in life and are also ready to part with their souls. Thus, souls aren't worth much because there's a surplus of them on the market.

If they can't sell their souls outright, many people think deception and cheating are expedient ways to achieve wealth, power, or fame. Our rational minds may ask, "What harm is there in taking a few moral liberties now and then so we can stiff some sucker for a few bucks?" The answer is: There will be a great deal of harm done in due time.

In simple terms, the best policy is to be impeccably committed to honesty regardless of the opportunities we may have to gain money, power, or fame through lying, cheating, and deception. Integrity is the foundation of quality relationships with friends, relatives, spouses, and business associates. So in order for you to get maximum satisfaction out of personal and professional relationships, it's imperative that you maintain your personal honor and good character.

Too often it's extremely tempting to get involved in something that will compromise your integrity. It should go without saying that you should contemptuously reject any such temptation — because compromising your integrity for money, power, or fame will come back to haunt you big time.

First, we shouldn't let our dishonest acts to run rampant because of the law of karma: What we do to others will eventually come back to us in some form or another. On this point alone, we should be committed to total honesty, even when it means our short-term success could suffer.

There is also the issue of our need to be true to ourselves. Values are only worth something when they are rigidly acted upon and followed at all times. This requires that we be as scrupulously honest as we can be with all people. The payoff is peace of mind and the satisfaction that we didn't have to resort to swindling someone to achieve our success in life.

Moral excellence should be your standard, with no justification for straying from this standard. Contrary to popular belief, there is a problem with telling just a few lies here and there. There will come a time when no one believes you even when you are telling the truth, because you have told one lie too many. Friedrich Nietzsche expressed it so well: "What upsets me is not that you lied to me, but that from now on I can no longer believe you." Cicero said basically the same thing: "A liar is not believed even though he tells the truth."

Always do the right and honest thing, regardless of how much more difficult it may appear to be. In the long term, it will be the easier and more rewarding thing to have done. The lust for success and money destroys more character than is justified. Earn your money and achieve success through service to others and not at the expense of others. When you look in the mirror, you already see the biggest troublemaker in your life — you don't want to also see a crook.

Take care of your reputation because it is important for your success and happiness. Once you deviate from what is right, you will have a difficult time making your way back again. Compromising your integrity just once can lead you to compromising it again and again — until you have nothing left to compromise. As already noted, you will end up losing your reputation and the trust of others. What's more, you will lose your self-respect — the greatest loss of all!

84
There Are Many Fascinating
Worlds Without Money

Money. Money. Money. Practically everyone aspires to having piles of money. Clearly, nothing else in the Western world is perceived to be as precious as money.

Money touches every area of our lives to some degree. The amount of money we have at our disposal can affect the quality of our relationships, friendships, housing, leisure, and health. If we use our imaginations, we can think of an unlimited number of ways in which we can use financial resources to add comfort and pleasure to our lives.

Yet for all its wondrous powers money can be terribly disappointing. This directly contradicts a basic axiom that guides nearly all human behavior — the axiom that the more money we have, the happier we will be.

Fact is, money is what you make it. Depending upon who you are — and your frame of mind — money can be anything you want it to be. Money can be the root of all evil or that which answers all things or something that burns a hole in your pocket or a means to freedom or an interesting concept — or even a stupid concept!

So what is money to you? Taking some time to create your own special definition will put you in better touch with money. Whatever your answer, congratulations! According to Zen masters, you are neither right nor wrong. Again, money is what you make it.

Whatever value you place on money, you must take responsibility for it. If money is evil to you, you created it being evil. If money is a problem to you, you created it being a problem. If money is joy to you, you created this concept. Take responsibility for your concepts. And be clear that these are just concepts — nothing more and nothing less.

Aha, concepts! How concepts tend to control our lives. The problem is, most concepts aren't reality. These concepts are illusions. Illusions take many forms — a fantastic plan, an erroneous belief, or an extraordinary desire.

Confusing illusions with reality isn't the way to freedom. To fill one's life with these illusions — especially about money — is to fill one's life with grief.

Look closely around you. You will see many people with a lot fewer financial resources than you have. Yet some of these people are much happier than you. Your thoughts may be, "I am sane; therefore, these people must be crazy." Maybe. Maybe not. Perhaps it's the other way around.

At the same time you will find people with a lot more money than you have who are not as happy as you. Again, you may think, "These people must be crazy." It's likely that they are not crazy. They just haven't found a way to be happy with all the wealth that they have because there is much more to happiness than wealth.

This is difficult for most people to grasp: Money doesn't talk; it just whispers. A large amount of financial resources solves all problems — except for all those it doesn't solve. And for the biggest disbelievers, a lot of cash at hand tends to create a few really big problems that weren't there before.

Money is neither good nor evil. There is nothing wrong with having a lot of money. Just don't expect it to guarantee contentment and peace of mind. The less happiness you expect to get from money, the more benefit you will be able to get out of it.

An old Italian proverb advises: "Make money your devoted servant; otherwise, it will be an overbearing master." In other words, learn to control money or it will control you. The novelist Henry Fielding said the same thing using different words: "If you make money your god, it will plague you like the devil."

There are three little known rules of money that can help you place it in better perspective: (1) If money becomes your primary focus in life, then money is all that you will get. (2) The person with no money may be poor, but not as poor as the person who has nothing but money. (3) Abundance isn't a matter of acquiring how much money you desire; it's a matter of being happy with how much you presently have.

If you are feeling unhappy, even though you are considered well-off by your friends, you don't need more financial resources. What you gravely need is more creative spirit in your soul. You may also need a whack on the side of the head from a Zen master!

Here are three more little known rules of money that will help you have a better relationship with it: (1) It's better to be out of money than out of new creative ideas on how to make money. (2) Spending a lot of money will get you trapped into thinking you are having a good time when all you are doing is spending a lot of money. (3) All things considered, the value of money lies in the creative and spiritual uses to which it can be put and not in how many possessions it can buy.

If you constantly have financial problems, you must accept that there is no special talent required in order to master money. Just earn your money before you spend it — and save at least 10 percent before you spend the rest of it. Follow this simple principle and you will have fewer financial difficulties than the vast majority of humankind. You will also show a maturity that most adults fail to achieve throughout their entire lives.

Above all, remember that there are many fascinating worlds without money. Don't make your life goal making the most money that you can. Instead, make your life goal making the most out of life that you can — regardless of how much money you have or earn. This will show that you have learned to love and cherish yourself and your dreams.

85

More Money Won't Bring You More Happiness — It Works the Other Way Around!

To most people in Western countries, a large amount of money is deemed an essential ingredient for happiness. For this reason, it's important that money and its relationship to happiness be put in proper perspective. Money is an important element for comfort and enjoyment of the finer things in life, but how much cash people need to be happy is another matter.

Money can do a lot for us, but we allow it to have too much control over our lives. The problem is that most of us don't acknowledge the truth about money. Some of us may not know the truth, and we don't want to hear it. Some of us know the truth deep down, but are in denial about it.

Most of us cling dearly to our beliefs, attitudes, and assumptions about money regardless of how much contradictory evidence the world brings our way. Accepting the truth would destroy the fantasy that acquiring a lot of financial resources will save us. Denying the truth about money keeps us locked into an unhealthy relationship with it and impedes our enjoyment of life.

Although our relationship with money changes as our circumstances and personal outlook change, we don't spend enough time contemplating the true value of money. Money can take on a different meaning when we think about it from a more spiritual or Zen perspective. After we ponder money in new ways, we may even find that many aspects of it are absurd. We may end up agreeing with George Bernard Shaw: "To be clever enough to get a great deal of money, one must be stupid enough to want it."

Contrary to public belief, earning a higher income or having more savings can be a trap that leads to a diminished quality of life. More cash often leads to more spending on material possessions; these items require a lot of one's time and more money for their maintenance. Of course, if the items have been purchased on credit, there is the pain of having to make even more money to make the payments in order to avoid personal bankruptcy.

More money should bring more freedom and more security instead of more slavery and more worry. Yet research studies indicate that financial prominence can bring its own form of hassles and worries. More money leads to alienation from previous peer groups, the pain of having to lose a lot more of one's assets in divorce, and more acute feelings of fear of someone stealing one's property and money.

Weirdly, there is a certain luxury in not having a large portfolio. I discovered that having financial assets can be somewhat of a burden. Managing my nest egg is frustrating and time consuming. Where do I put it? How often should I change my investment strategy? (Don't ask me for my cash and other financial resources, however. It's not as troublesome looking after my nest egg as it would be for me to give it to you.)

Clearly, we all need money but the pursuit of wealth can cost us precious time and, more important, our independence. One reason people pursue the almighty dollar zealously is that they make an absurd assumption about money. Although many wise people over the ages have warned us that money can't buy happiness, most of us ignore this wisdom. We strive for happiness that is supposed to accompany increased wealth regardless of the required sacrifices. The belief system that more money can bring more happiness needs some severe auditing.

Here is the bottom line: Money, generally speaking, can't buy what your heart truly desires nor can it buy what you can't see. Yet what your heart truly desires and what you can't see are fundamental to being happy. In this group you can list peace of mind, love, job satisfaction, and spiritual fulfillment. Many rich people don't have these elements of happiness and, regardless of their financial prominence, they can't buy these things.

Even health can't be bought. No doubt financial might can provide better quality healthcare, particularly in the United States, where public healthcare is not universal as it is in Canada. Once you destroy great health, however, you can't buy it back. Right living and enjoyable work — and not the almighty dollar and material possessions — are ingredients of great health.

If you were to think about it for a while, you would realize that there are many more personal attributes contributing to happiness that are beyond the realm of money. Besides the ones already cited, you would likely add real friends, a sense of humor, good character, self-reliance, integrity, personal creativity, self-esteem, and emotional stability to your list — not to mention a good night's sleep.

If all these are ingredients of happiness, and they can't be bought, then it follows that happiness can't be bought with cash. When you finally accept this, it is much easier to break the relationship between happiness and money. Of course, if we are extremely poor (starving or homeless), more money can bring a much better life.

Beyond a certain level — not as high as we may think — more money doesn't translate into more happiness, however. In fact, it works the other way around — more happiness will bring more money! Put another way, first learn how to be happy with little or no money and money will come much more easily in your life.

Ludicrous, no? Let's go back to the above-mentioned ingredients of happiness that can't be bought. I assure you that if you take time to develop all these ingredients, you will be one happy camper. What's more, virtually every one of these elements will help you earn more money.

Clearly, if you are already in possession of all these elements of happiness, you are well-qualified — better than the vast majority in society — to earn a great income. If you aren't in possession of these elements of happiness, develop them and you will end up with what it takes to make a lot more money — even if you no longer need a lot of money to be happy.

86

True Prosperity Is Living Easily and Happily Whether You Have Lots of Money or Not

In an overly materialistic world, prosperity is unfortunately and invariably associated with hoards of money and countless possessions. Yet to the truly prosperous people of this world, prosperity is prosperity in its purest and original sense. Prosperity comes from the Latin word *spes*, which means "hope and vigor." To the truly prosperous person, being prosperous means being positive and happy in the moment.

Clearly, true prosperity is living easily and happily whether you have lots of money or not. I have had the fortune of being on both sides of the fence. I have been broke, over $30,000 in debt, and have had to borrow money to pay the rent. At one time I even had the sobering experience of sleeping in my car for two cold winter nights when the temperature was -21° F. Extremely cold, of course, but this is still far from the bottom. As Mike Todd said, "I've never been poor, only broke. Being poor is a state of mind. Being broke is a temporary situation."

Many years later I am fortunate enough to have a good income, spending substantially less money than I earn and investing a nice surplus each year. Having been broke on more than one occasion makes me a lot more grateful for the financial position I enjoy today. Yet I often felt just as prosperous — even more prosperous at certain times — when I was broke as I do today.

For instance, the year I wrote my international bestseller *The Joy of Not Working* I was in debt big time, but I was filled with hope and vigor, the true feeling of prosperity. I recall telling a few people that I had a good sense about the book and "it may just make me a million dollars." For the record, to date the book has earned me about half that amount and it still gives me a nice residual income whether I am awake or asleep. This would not have been possible if I hadn't felt prosperous enough to take up writing and self-publishing when I had no savings and little income.

Spiritual leaders say that as a matter of course prosperity will come when you are pursuing the right things with your life. To feel truly prosperous, you may have to leave the corporate world for good simply because prosperity and freedom go hand in hand. For some people this means having to give up a substantial amount of their income, at least for a certain period of time.

Most people are too afraid to give up a secure job because they don't think that they have what it takes to leave the corporate world. False beliefs about your limitations will hold you back from gaining freedom. No complaining and no victim stuff. Okay? The more loving your personality and the more love you have for life and your work, the more money you will attract and the more you will enjoy spending the money.

So, as long as you believe, without doubt, in your prosperity, then you will experience a world in which you are prosperous and free of money worries. Consciously worrying about money or being subconsciously motivated by the fear of running out of money hardly ever produces great wealth. Trust that you will always have enough money to get by, even if you quit your lousy job to pursue your dream career.

Indeed, your prosperity will grow to the extent that you do. Your feeling of prosperity may require that you overcome the fear of leaving a secure job for a less secure job, with less pay, but a lot more freedom. Fact is, feeling more prosperous doesn't necessarily mean earning more money. Sometimes it means earning less money.

Contrary to popular belief, prosperity is an emotional state that has little to do with your wealth or the state of the economy. You can feel more prosperous in a one-room cottage than most wealthy people feel in a twenty-room mansion. Misers will hoard a lot of money and spendthrifts will spend whatever they have — you don't have to do either to feel prosperous. You may have to give up your secure, high-paying corporate job, however — and grow spiritually in the process.

87
Financial Insanity Has Its Own Big Following — Including You and Me

As already discussed, it's a lot easier to avoid trouble than to get out of trouble. Yet most of us go to great extremes to invite trouble into our lives. Mishandling money is one of our favorite ways to get ourselves into difficulty. We seem to forget that each spending choice we make determines how much money we need in our lives — and how hard we have to work for it.

Unfortunately, money is more often misused and abused than used intelligently. Most people haven't figured out how to use money wisely to truly enhance their lives. Most, it seems, act rationally with their money only when they can't dream up any more irrational ways to spend it. Clearly, financial insanity has developed its own big following — including you and me.

The problem is that our spending habits don't represent our deepest values and desires. We waste our funds on questionable material possessions at the expense of things that we cherish, such as freedom and financial independence. We may meticulously save for a sabbatical or retirement, for example, but then, after a year or two, blow the entire $10,000 in a moment of weakness on a new stereo system — which we hardly use, because we don't have time for it. Alternatively, we may buy a new wardrobe that falls out of fashion in one season.

If you believe that you are beyond dysfunctional financial behavior, you are probably in denial. Perhaps a strange and confusing relationship exists between how hard you work to earn your money and how easily you spend it at times. You may pinch pennies when buying food at the market on payday, but later blow what's left on gadgets that you could easily do without.

In fact, many people spend most of their paychecks on the best junk money can buy. Worse, they tend to buy this junk with money they haven't yet earned. Will Rogers said this so eloquently: "Too many people spend money they haven't earned, to buy things they don't want, to impress people they don't like." Although we won't admit it, each of us exhibits a little bit of this insanity.

Money, unfortunately, brings out the eccentricity in each of us. An occasional quirk or peculiarity in our spending habits is normal. But consistent irrational behavior with money is detrimental to our personal and financial well-being. Indeed, 93 percent of retired Americans end up dependent on some form of social security because they haven't learned the art of saving money.

Modifying serious irrational monetary behavior requires effort; otherwise, financial problems will continue to interfere with our leading a happy and fulfilling life. At the source, most irrational financial behavior is not really about money at all. Financial behavior goes deeper than money itself.

Miguel de Cervantes advised, "Make it thy business to know thyself, which is the most difficult lesson in the world." Knowing yourself and what drives you to spend your money — whether it's cars, homes, fashions, or cool stuff — is essential to having total control of your finances. This can be the difference between having a million dollars for retirement and having nothing.

More often than not, things that people purchase impulsively end up giving them little pleasure and don't enhance their lives in any way. Just a little critical thought can prevent this from happening to you. If you question the true value of every service or item you purchase, the number of your purchases will go down dramatically.

This technique requires that you ask questions about every intended purchase to be absolutely clear whether it serves a real need or a true personal want. By meticulously asking questions, you will find that you don't really need or want most of the things that capture your interest. Besides building wealth, you will enjoy life when you stop wasting time and money on things that don't bring you pleasure and satisfaction.

All things considered, your best purchases will turn out to be the ones that you never make. Getting in touch with the emotional quirks that drive your irrational spending can save you hundreds of thousands of dollars over the next decade or two. This means that you will have to work only half as hard as the general population to lead a full, relaxed, happy, and satisfying life.

88

Spend More Money on Your Personal Development than on Your Next Hairstyle

Most people in Western society have no qualms about utilizing hard-earned money — and often going into debt big time — for the latest furniture, clothing, cars, and electronic goods. They will even purchase gadgets and trinkets that add absolutely nothing to their happiness and satisfaction. But will they part with some of their cash for educational products that could help them become more successful in life? It has been my experience that over 95 percent won't.

If you have never done this, attend a two- or three-day motivational event sometime soon. One thing will stand out among the array of successful and polished speakers: They all will say that their success and polish is due to the books they have read, the seminars they have taken, and the mentors with whom they have worked. Surprisingly, most will also admit that they were miserable failures early in their lives.

Take, for example, John Assaraf. He was the leader of a street gang when he was nineteen. Assaraf wanted to change his life but he didn't know how. "I got a job selling real estate," says Assaraf, "and fortunately someone took me to a sales training seminar." He has spent over $500,000 on seminars and coaching in the twenty-five years since then. It seems like a fortune — and it is until you learn that his current net worth is over $1 billion! The return on Assaraf's investment in education has been approximately 2,000 percent.

If you want to be more successful in life, spend more on your personal development than on your next hairstyle. It was the irreverent Jeff Foxworthy who stated, "You may be a redneck if you have spent more on your pickup truck than on your education." Redneck or not, you should be spending a certain percentage of your income on your career advancement, self-education, and personal development.

Harv Eker, author of *Secrets of the Millionaire Mind*, advises that you should allocate 10 percent of your after-tax income to self-education. My take on the 10-percent figure is this could be a touch high, particularly if you earn over a million dollars a year. I have allocated 5 percent of my after-tax income to my personal and business education, which works well for me.

Whether through a book, a magazine article, a seminar, travel to another country, or a conversation with a truly successful person, whatever it is that you undertake, always look to broaden your experiences and your education. This applies regardless of how many college or university degrees you have to your name. "Formal education will make you a living; self-education will make you a fortune," according to Jim Rohn.

It has been my experience that the right educational products such as motivational books, seminars, and CDs can be much more valuable than an MBA for achieving success at what I do. I should know. I have an MBA and have found virtually no material worth reviewing from the courses I took in the program. Yet I find motivational books, seminars, and CDs great resources for reminding me what helped me become successful as an author and publisher.

Of course, you should not take all career and personal development advice as gospel. You do not need to take the techniques to extremes nor do you have to do everything suggested. Advice reflects one particular person's truth and view of the world. Take whatever useful ideas you need from career and personal development material. Every book, seminar, or coaching session should have at least one important tool, strategy, or insight. Take what appeals to you and run with it. At the same time discard what doesn't work for you.

Your creative mind is your greatest asset and you should be spending money to enhance it. Regardless of the amount you allocate for your career and personal development, this overall point is important: The money you put in your education account is an investment in yourself that can reap unbelievable returns. Search out the best tools available to open up your creative side, get you focused, and direct you toward attaining true success. These tools may cost you a tidy sum at the outset, but they will save you time and make you a lot more money in the long run.

89

To Have a Good Grasp of Money, Try Joyfully Parting with a Fair Portion of It!

Paradoxically, the most important thing that money can help provide is personal freedom — but earning or having a lot of money is not necessarily liberating to everyone. Although not a problem for most people, particularly today's North Americans, it is all too easy for some of us to fall into the trap of spending too little money. Once we have worked hard or smart for many years to create an independent income, it follows that we should be enjoying a portion of it.

To have a good grasp of money, try joyfully parting with a fair portion of it! This is the only way money can add to the feeling of prosperity. Preposterous as it may seem, countless people in elite income brackets have proven that financial independence doesn't necessarily mean prosperity. Many misers have put together a great fortune and have not experienced one bit of pleasure or joy out of spending a portion. Talk about financial dysfunction!

If you can afford it, but still feel afraid to spend money for something you truly want, keep in mind that money is a means and not an end. Prosperity spending is good for your financial soul. Enjoying your money, provided you have truly earned it and haven't borrowed it, will motivate you to produce more. You will also have learned how to appreciate your money so that you can really enjoy yourself when you acquire much more money from one of your creative projects.

If it's a crushing experience to spend money for something you would like and can easily afford, you haven't gained freedom — you have psychologically imprisoned yourself. What good is having a lot of money if you still do tasks that you hate? In fact, living ridiculously below your means is just as financially dysfunctional as living way above your means. Staying in a dive by choice, and no longer by necessity, doesn't make much sense. This is definitely a sign of poverty-consciousness and not prosperity-consciousness.

The feeling of prosperity is available to you whenever you want it. Feeling prosperous means paying your utility bills on time and with a smile on your face. Prosperity means not only giving to the homeless person, but being cheerful when you do it. Prosperity also means buying fresh produce with a feeling of gratitude instead of buying day-old bread or bargain overripe fruit with a scowl on your face. Still more, being prosperous means tipping generously with glee when the waiter has given you great service instead of trying to stiff him with a mere 5 percent — or worse, no tip at all.

Even when you aren't earning a great deal of money, it's important at least once a week to do something to reward yourself — to feel prosperous and deserving of money. With a healthy and balanced attitude toward spending and saving, enjoying your money in the present will help you accumulate more in the future. Sacrificing all your disposable money for savings, and not enjoying a portion of it today on pleasure, is actually an act of stealing from yourself. It is unlikely that you will enjoy your money even if you become a multimillionaire.

I would advise that you create a prosperity account that is separate from your financial-independence account. Allot 5 to 10 percent of your net income for things that you want but don't need. Ensure that you deplete your prosperity account every six months or so and spend every penny in this account on your pleasure. Don't be afraid to spend this money frivolously. When you can afford it, the money you enjoy spending frivolously is spent well.

Although money can't buy happiness, it can add to your enjoyment of life — which is the reason for having financial independence in the first place. Prosperity in itself will come when you are pursuing the right things in your life. These include not only being in the right career, but also spending money on the right things and saving enough to accumulate a nest egg for sabbaticals, retirement, and emergencies.

Money will be your friend — like all friends — only if you treat it with respect. Money requires that you save it prudently and spend it joyfully. Treat it with disrespect, and you will always have financial problems — or suffer from poverty-consciousness — regardless of how much money you make.

90
Being a Success at Work Is Irrelevant
If You Are a Failure at Home

Perhaps you are like millions of people in today's world whose need to make a good living has gotten out of hand and become an obsession. You yearn for more excitement, more adventure, more satisfaction, and more happiness. Clearly, if you are leading an unhealthy lifestyle to earn more and more money, you are poor no matter how much you earn.

The universe defies you to answer the following four questions: (1) What good is a high-paying career if it leaves you continually stressed out and miserable? (2) What good is owning a larger house than average if the only time you spend in it is when you sleep in it? (3) What good is having a lot of interesting possessions if you never have the free time to enjoy any? (4) Above all, what good is having a family if you seldom see any of its members?

One thing is certain: Being a success at work is irrelevant if you are a failure at home. Sure, success is relative. But it encompasses all aspects of life — work, family, friends, leisure activities, artistic pursuits, and mental, physical, and spiritual health. Not surprisingly, researchers have found that individuals who find the time to do the things they enjoy are much happier and live longer than people who just plod on with their work and regular routines at the expense of personal life.

You won't be prosperous until you sleep enough, eat well, exercise regularly, and spend sufficient time with friends and family. It's possible to be a huge success at work and miss out on life completely. You shouldn't be sacrificing present joy, happiness, and satisfaction for a few extra lousy bucks, especially if you are going to spend the money frivolously on some gadgets that won't enhance your life significantly. Day-to-day life will have little meaning if your main reason for going to work is to pay for all those possessions you don't have time to use.

What's the point of being well-off financially if there's no time to truly live — but only exist? "Perpetual devotion to what a man calls his business," reflected Robert Louis Stevenson, "is only to be sustained by neglect of many other things." Rest and constructive leisure activities are half of what you need for a life of purpose and accomplishment. Friends, family, adventure, walking, meditating, creative loafing, and spiritual fulfillment — not working long and hard hours — are the things that make life worth living.

The richest people in the world are those who have fun earning their living and at the same time have a healthy work/life balance. Individuals with an excellent work/life balance have set their priorities right. Only you can decide whether you have your priorities right and are living according to them. You have to be completely clear about the type and quality of life you want to live. The degree to which you put time and effort into the things that really matter will determine your overall happiness and satisfaction.

While making life-altering changes to create a balanced lifestyle isn't easy, millions have shown it is possible. They have gotten their emotional acts together and accomplished what the majority have not. It is no wonder that these people live happier and fuller lives by spending more time with family, connecting with nature and the community, and enjoying the many simple pleasures that they had forgotten in pursuit of the good life.

It's easy to believe that the system makes you work long and hard hours. Be clear that the system does not enslave people — people enslave themselves. If you do not accept this, you have given away your creative power for the perverse satisfaction of being enslaved. Denial will prevent you from making the changes that can make a real difference in your life.

The paramount question you have to ask yourself is: Which is more important — making a good living or making a good life? You must know the moment when to work diligently. Even more essential, you must know the moment when not to work, but to relax and play instead. This will not only benefit your family and you immensely — but will also astonish most of your friends and colleagues.

91
The Work Ethic Is a
Terrible Mistake

Although imagination, perseverance, dedication, commitment, and action are important ingredients for achieving true success, it may come as a surprise — to a few people at least — that hard work is not one of them. By hard work I mean working strenuously, for long hours, and on as many tasks and projects as possible. Plain and simple, hard work and true success — oil and water! Put another way, hard work and true success don't mix all that well.

True success, in fact, is about working smart and not hard. Personally, the only time I am a big fan of hard work is when someone else is doing it and I am paying for it. This is not to say that I won't work hard at times, particularly on productive projects that excite me, or ones that I must complete within a certain time frame. But I find most hard work detrimental to my well-being.

Contrary to popular belief, the work ethic is a terrible mistake — a cute term gone haywire! It is promoted most vehemently either by employers who want to exploit pathetic workaholics or by pathetic workaholics themselves who are trying to justify why they work so many hours and have no real life.

As is to be expected, everything worthwhile has a price. There is a price for not working hard enough; there is an even larger price for working too hard. Of course, corporations would like you to believe that "hard work is good for you and it never harmed anyone." There are reasons to believe otherwise, however.

According to a 2002 study in the *British Medical Journal*, employees with stressful jobs are twice as likely to die from heart disease as those who have jobs with little or no stress. What's more, employees who work over forty-eight hours per week double their risk of heart disease, according to a 1996 UK government report. Still more, according to a 2003 American study, long-term job strain is worse for your heart than gaining forty pounds in weight or aging thirty years. Not to mention that approximately two million workers die annually due to occupational injuries and illnesses, according to one United

Nations report. This means that work kills more people than war (650,000 deaths per year).

Contrary to popular belief, hard work can kill you. Another dark side of the work ethic is how many rainbow-chasers end up working hard all their lives, expecting success, but with nothing to show for it. The key to true success, in fact, is to work on the few things that are truly important and make a difference in this world, and to disregard the rest. In this regard, management consultant and university professor Peter Drucker advised, "Do the right things instead of trying to do everything right."

Clearly, if you are channeling your hard work into areas that offer little chance for big payoffs, your hard work will likely be in vain. On the other hand, if you work only four or five hours a day at creative endeavors that offer the likelihood of immense payoffs, four or five hours a day may be all that you need to hit it big so that you can live a comfortable life. Even two or three hours a day can do the trick in the developed world, with so much opportunity.

The key is not to overdo things. Pablo Picasso was one of the most prolific and influential artists of the twentieth century. No doubt you will agree that Picasso, who excelled in painting, sculpture, etching, stage design, and ceramics, attained an impressive measure of real success as an artist. Yet Picasso, like me, did not believe in being an achiever at all costs.

"You must always work not just within but below your means," claimed Picasso. "If you can handle three elements, handle only two. If you can handle ten, then handle only five. In that way the ones you do handle, you handle with more ease, more mastery, and you create a feeling of strength in reserve."

Suffice it to say that creativity ultimately produces the biggest payoffs. Although both creative effort and hard work require action, the former is at the heart of true success. The latter has been known to lead to nervous twitching, heart attacks, and dubious results. Taking this into account, there is no greater joy than experiencing a great work/life balance by working only four to eight hours a day — except, perhaps, the joy of watching workaholics working ten or more hours a day fully engaged in their reckless pursuit of insanity.

92

Work As Hard As You Have to for a Comfortable Living — and As Little As You Can Get Away With

It is possible to have a lifestyle that coincides with your deepest values if you really want it. Taking control of your life starts with you — not with your employer, the government, your spouse, or society. You can choose whether you want to opt out of excessive work and materialism for a life that includes more leisure and time to relax, more time with your kids, and more rewarding work.

Clearly, if you are working more than eight hours a day, you are in the wrong job. Either that — or you are doing it wrong! If anything can help you get your life in proper balance, it's the 80/20 rule, first discovered by Italian economist Vilfredo Pareto more than one hundred years ago. Following this rule is incredibly powerful for dealing with a time crunch and avoiding the workaholism that has afflicted much of the world.

Generally speaking, the 80/20 rule tells us that in any area of life a few activities (approximately 20 percent) are vital and many activities (approximately 80 percent) are trivial. The key is to focus our time and energy on the 20 percent of our work projects, friends, investments, and leisure activities that are really important. In regards to work, the first 80 percent of our results will come from the first 20 percent of our time and effort. This leaves only 20 percent of our results that are attained from the remaining 80 percent of our time and effort.

Perhaps you have read one or more of the many articles written about the 80/20 rule, but like many people who know about it, you don't fully utilize it for its remarkable potential. You are likely wondering: If the 80/20 rule is so effective, why doesn't everyone use it? The answer, quite simply, is that it requires creative thinking, and it requires being different and unconventional. These two requirements keep the majority of people from using it because the majority of people are trying to fit in with the majority of people — they are too afraid to be different.

What is really cool is that 80/20 thinking can help you achieve much more with much less effort. You can work less, earn more money, and enjoy your personal life like never before. As a bonus, utilizing the 80/20 rule day in and day out can make you wealthy over the long term.

The power to decide what activities are important and the commitment to focus on these activities are basic to having a balanced lifestyle. "Things that matter most," said Johann Wolfgang von Goethe, "must never be at the mercy of things that matter least." Clearly, most of what we do in life has low value in regards to our happiness and satisfaction.

Given the high probability that you spend 80 percent of your time on low-priority activities, you must reassess how much time you want to spend on these activities. To make optimum use of your time, get rid of the 80 percent of activities that give you only 20 percent of your results. You may not be able to do away with all these activities, but you can do away with many. If you can eliminate at least half of your low-value activities, you will create more time to pursue other important things in life, including a lot more leisure time.

You must identify where you get a lot more than you put in. Also pinpoint the areas where you get back a fraction of what you put in. The objective is to maximize the results from the areas of great surpluses and to bail out of those activities with big deficits. With the 80/20 rule as your most powerful tool, you can take creative liberties to live life the way you would like instead of the way the masses do. Not only will you create an excellent life/work balance, but you will find that work is much more pleasurable and satisfying — especially when you can produce a lot more results and money with a lot less effort and time.

For your life to work, and work well, you must apply the 80/20 rule ruthlessly in all areas of life. Eliminate unnecessary activities that offer little in benefits to your income, happiness, or satisfaction. Contrary to what society believes, hard work is the best thing ever invented for killing time — as well as you. The key to a full, relaxed, satisfying, and happy life is to work as hard as you have to for a comfortable living — and as little as you can get away with. The 80/20 rule allows you to accomplish this with ease and excellence.

93

It's Best to Leave Perfection for the Misfits of This World to Pursue

To have a full, relaxed, satisfying, and happy life, you must concentrate on the things that really matter. Still, caution is urged. Not only are most worthwhile things not worth doing well, but all things worth doing well are not worth overdoing. This is no different than cooking a fine meal. Important work shouldn't be underdone, but neither should it be overdone.

Many people strive for perfection — which is the first rung of the ladder that leads to failure. Doing things with perfection in mind involves trying to achieve what can't be done. It invariably leads to the inefficient and ineffective use of one's limited resources. Moreover, the results are often dubious at best.

Excellence is what you should strive for given that perfection and excellence are very different. Doing things in excellence means doing your best with the time, energy, and other resources you have available. This leads to quality results achieved through effective and efficient use of limited resources.

Allow me to share a personal example: When I started writing my best-selling book *The Joy of Not Working* on January 1 of the year it was written, I allowed myself until July 31 to complete the first draft of the manuscript. After I beat my deadline by one day, I gave myself another month in which to have several friends review the manuscript and suggest changes.

After making all the changes within the available time, I got my book to the printer and had it self-published by September 15. By keeping to my to-printer deadline, I was able to introduce the book to the bookstore market well in advance of the competition and get more publicity before the all-important Christmas shopping season, in large part because it was published sooner.

After the book had sold over 30,000 copies, making it a Canadian bestseller for three straight years, I decided to update the book. This time, I used an updated version of my word processing program, which now had a spell-check. Surprise! The original edition of my book had 150 spelling errors.

Did this hurt sales? Near as I can tell, not very much — if at all.

The point is, if I wanted to get everything in the book perfect, I would still be working on it over fifteen years later. On the other hand, writing and self-publishing the book in excellence — even though it was far from perfect — allowed me to bring out a book that has become an international bestseller and has provided me with a nice residual income for over fifteen years.

It may come as a surprise to many, but pursuing perfection on important projects is just as harmful as settling for mediocrity. Both lead to dissatisfaction, unhappiness, and a lack of true success. "A lot of disappointed people," warned Donald Kennedy, "have been left standing on the street corner waiting for the bus marked 'Perfection.' "

Like everyone else in this world, you may at times get bit by the perfection bug. Remember that no perfectly published book, no perfectly prepared meal, no perfectly written report, or no perfectly satisfied customer exists. You should resist the urge to attain perfection in any area of your life just as you should resist the urge to be mediocre in something important to you. You shouldn't end up feeling as though you failed to get things right or fell short of what others might accomplish.

The key is to strive for excellence, which is somewhere between mediocrity and perfection. You must decide where excellence falls. Loosely stated, excellence is putting in the best effort you can with the time, energy, and other resources you have available. Keep in mind, however, that you don't have to do anything flawlessly to be highly successful.

It's best to leave perfection for the misfits of this world to pursue. Paradoxically, the one thing that prevents many people from being really good at an activity related to work or play is their trying to be too good at it. Clearly, nothing can be a greater waste of human spirit than trying to live up to the unattainable standard of perfection.

94
Most Activities Worth Doing Should Be Done in the Most Haphazardly Fashion Possible

Many underlying factors are a hindrance to success. Surprisingly, you would think that excellence is not one of them — but the opposite is true. The pursuit of excellence, in fact, can hinder your having a full, relaxed, satisfying, and happy life just as much as the pursuit of perfection.

One of the best ways to complicate your existence is to believe in the old adage that "anything worth doing is worth doing well." If you believe this nonsense, you've struck out even before you step out of the dugout on the way to the batter's box. You will invest an inordinate amount of time, energy, and even money on tasks and projects that end up being an exercise in tedium, with hardly any return to you.

Fact is, doing the wrong things in excellence won't get you much success in life. If the key ingredient of your business is telephoning your clients, for example, you should concentrate most of your efforts on this activity. Spending six or seven hours cleaning your desk in excellence and five minutes making phone calls won't be one-tenth as productive as spending one or two hours making phone calls and five minutes cleaning your desk. In the less productive case, you will have worked six hours and five minutes, whereas you will have worked only one hour and five minutes in the much more productive case.

Real success demands that you do your best in the time you have available, but this advice comes with a qualification: The key is to do your best at the important things and do far from your best at the unimportant things. People who learn to strive for excellence in a few really important things — instead of striving for a great performance in everything — are able to turn their lives around 180 degrees.

The key is paying attention. Refuse to get sidetracked by low-priority projects. The fact that some task is interesting doesn't mean that pursuing it is worthwhile. Even if the activity is helpful, this still doesn't make doing it well worthwhile. The question is, how much does it help? In other words, is it more helpful than other projects you could be pursuing?

In fact, you may want to go one step further and ask yourself whether the project has to be done at all. Surprisingly, many people focus on work projects and other activities that make absolutely no contribution to their success. After all, it doesn't matter how active you are if you don't know the true purpose of your activity. Whenever you are working on the wrong things, no matter how much you work, you will never do enough.

If you are a peak performer, you will have learned that there are three ways to handle a task fast: (1) Do it yourself. (2) Hire someone to handle it for you. (3) Decide that it isn't worth doing and strike it off your to-do list. Doing things in excellence can be productive, without doubt. Avoiding doing certain things can be even more productive, however.

If you decide that the task is worth doing, to repeat, you must not be intimidated by "Anything worth doing is worth doing well." This is one of the most ridiculous statements ever made. Fact is, most things worth doing aren't worth your best efforts. There are just a few really important activities that are worth doing well.

After that, a greater number of things are worth doing adequately. What's more, most activities worth doing should be done in the most haphazardly fashion possible just so that you can get by. Of course, most things aren't worth doing at all, and are best left for the misfits of this world to pursue.

Thus, choose your activities wisely. Spend your time and energy on the important few instead of the insignificant many. Once you have this mastered, you will achieve success and happiness beyond your wildest dreams.

After all, people who observe no limits in attempting to get as many tasks done as possible in excellence aren't nearly as smart as they think. A lot of work can be done by any fool. But to be highly productive and successful while doing just a few select tasks and still have plenty of time to rest and play — this is where true genius resides.

95

If You Are What You Ain't, Then You Ain't What You Truly Should Be

In the midst of it all we are all driven by a few typically human motivations. One of them is our desire for freedom. The freedom that deep down most of us are looking for is the freedom to be ourselves — the freedom to pursue what we truly want and not what someone else wants us to want. Unfortunately, most of the time we do things to please others — to be accepted by others — instead of living our lives to please ourselves.

In an attempt to please others, most people try to fit in with the crowd. Perhaps you are one of them. You may take comfort in knowing that you are in the large majority of people who follow the herd regardless of where it goes. After all, it is easier to follow the herd than to think differently and do things on your own.

You will always follow the herd at your peril, however. The problem with herds is that they occasionally start stampedes that are hard to stop. And when a herd causes a lot of damage, none of its members is willing to take responsibility.

Clearly, far too few people in this world think for themselves. Instead of allowing their own creativity and inner wisdom to run their lives, they choose what others are doing. You don't have to be one of those people. As an active, creative-thinking human being, you should realize that — contrary to popular wisdom — you always have an alternative to following the herd. While the herd is moving in one direction, you can go in any of several other directions.

Following the majority as it looks for happiness in all the wrong places will not lead to anywhere worth going. Why waste time, energy, and money chasing after something you don't really need and may not even enjoy? Some things are important, and others are not. Some things appear to be important because people have been brainwashed by society, educational institutions, and advertisers to believe that they are important. Upon close scrutiny, most of these things have no relevance to having a happy and healthy lifestyle.

The more you question what the masses are doing, the more you will realize that the everybody-else-is-doing-it approach isn't the way to put your mark on this world. While it's tempting to join the masses, always remember that you have meaningful dreams and more important things to pursue.

It's best to stand above the crowd even if you have to stand alone. There is no greater way to gain self-respect and the respect of others in this world. Do what is right even when what a million others are doing is wrong. Plain and simple, even though a million people do a stupid thing, it still remains a stupid thing.

At the best of times, chasing after the approval of others by emulating them is a zero-results game. To be impressed by others and their possessions is to lose your true self. One of your most important goals in life should be to be you and not anyone else. When Leonardo da Vinci was asked what his greatest accomplishment had been in his life, he replied, "Leonardo da Vinci." Similarly, Zen masters don't ask us to be something or someone we aren't; instead, they ask us to be more truly and more fully who we are.

Being truly and fully who you are requires that you know what is important to you, and only you. You have to make sure that your life's choices are your own. To quote e. e. cummings, "To be nobody-but-yourself — in a world which is doing its best, night and day, to make you like everybody-else — means to fight the hardest battle any human being can fight; and never stop fighting."

All things considered, if you are what you ain't, then you ain't what you truly should be. You cannot be your true self by becoming a me-too person. When you become like everyone else, you may as well be no one. When you become a me-different person, you become a courageous and interesting person — an individual who knows what he or she truly wants out of life and ends up getting it.

96
You Can't Make a Big Difference in This World Unless You Are Different

All humans, when they are born, have one important thing in common — they are all different. Once schools, universities, corporations, and society do their damage, however, the majority of individuals spend most of their lives trying to be like everyone else. Even if this means being an average or an ordinary or an everyday or a run-of-the-mill human being, they give it their best shot. "The American ideal, after all," wrote American author James Baldwin, "is that everyone should be as much alike as possible."

There are a few things in life that work better in practice than in theory. Being different than others in society is one of them. Social theory says that we are social animals and must fit in with others to achieve success and happiness. Educational institutions, corporations, and society in general influence most people to conform and be like everyone else. Standing out in the crowd is considered subversive. Individuals who are different can end up being criticized and ridiculed by people who run with the pack.

Social theory overlooks an important aspect of human nature, unfortunately, while advocating the merits of our conforming and fitting in with the rest of society. We all want to leave a mark on this world. Put another way, we want to know that our life matters, that we make a difference somehow.

Many underlying factors help determine how much real success we attain and how much we affect others. But it's the creative people throughout the ages — the individuals willing to risk, be different, challenge the status quo, and ruffle a few feathers — who have made a big difference in this world. These are the individuals who achieve success, satisfaction, and happiness on a level not normally experienced by people who run with the pack.

You may have noticed that anything of major consequence in this world was initiated by characters who were different than the rest of society. In fact, they were out of step with society in large measure. Think Richard Branson!

Think Oprah Winfrey! Think Steven Jobs! Think Anita Roddick! If you want to be like these people, you must come to terms with the fact that fitting in with everyone else is not the way to achieve true success in this world.

Plain and simple: These individuals all made a big difference in this world because they were willing to be different. Richard Branson is considered a "flake" by much of the British business establishment — but do you think that Branson cares? Yet, unfortunately, most people are trying to fit in with colleagues at work, to be the same as everyone else in society, instead of being different and deviating from the normal, established, or expected.

The big lesson here is that you yourself can't make a big difference in this world unless you are different from the masses. Being different is the only way to be successful in your own right. Some people may be uncomfortable with you and others may dislike you for it. No doubt you will be criticized a lot. The more success you have at being different, the more you may be disliked. People will respect you for it, nonetheless, particularly when you start making that big difference. More fundamental and powerful, without question, you will have your own respect.

As long as you are trying to be like someone else, the best you can ever be is a carbon copy — and probably a poor one at that. This is exactly the type of behavior that keeps losers in the cycle of playing a losing game, that stops these same talented human beings from evolving into legends.

You, and only you, should determine who you truly are. If you resort to being your true self, you will be different. If this means that some people think you are eccentric, so be it. As John Crowe points out, "It takes a strong fish to swim against the current. Even a dead one can float with it."

Your chances for a financially rewarding and psychologically satisfying life will increase in direct proportion to how much you are willing to be out of step with the rest of the pack. The more unconventional you are, the better. After all, individuals such as Richard Branson who are different — even wildly eccentric — change the world. People who run with the pack — and are very ordinary — try to keep the world the way it is. Which would you rather be?

97
Look Inside and You Will Find More Outside

For centuries the great philosophers and spiritual leaders of this world have been telling the truth about happiness. They could shout it from the rooftops every day and cast it in every stone, however — and most people still wouldn't get it. True happiness emanates from the inside — not from the outside. Put another way, we can experience true happiness only by finding contentment within ourselves.

The Sufi religious sect has an age-old parable about the antics of the fool-saint Mullah Nasruddin that explains why so few of us ever find true happiness. As some neighbors of Mullah Nasruddin arrive home one dark evening, they see the Mullah digging under a street lamp in front of his house. "Mullah, whatever are you doing?" asks one of the neighbors.

"I'm looking for my keys which I have lost," replies the Mullah. Soon the neighbors are all helping him scratch about in the dirt under the street lamp, searching for his keys. After a while, another one of the neighbors speaks up: "We have spent quite a bit of time searching now. This is not working. Mullah, think back. Where did you last have your keys?" The Mullah replies: "Well, I lost them somewhere in the house, but I'm not sure where."

"What!" exclaims the bewildered neighbor. "Why are we searching out here then?" The Mullah answers, "Why? Because it is much too dark in the house. Can't you see that there is more light under the lamp?"

This parable is entertaining and at the same time thought-provoking; deeper esoteric teachings are part of Sufi parables such as this one. This parable, in fact, illustrates the folly of people looking to the external world for happiness and satisfaction instead of looking within.

Just as the Mullah won't find his keys outside his house, we won't find true happiness and enlightenment by searching in the external world, regardless of how bright it appears out there. After all, the key to happiness is locked inside ourselves, where it can be pretty dark at times.

To a great degree most of us spend way too much time looking to the external world for satisfaction and enlightenment. French writer Duc François de La Rochefoucauld wasn't kidding when he said, "A man who finds no satisfaction in himself, seeks for it in vain elsewhere."

Because most people are afraid to search inside themselves for true happiness, some spend their time enslaved by their possessions. Others take drugs or alcohol to keep the pace moving fast. Still others live vicariously through their false heroes. Yet no amount of external objects, affection, or attention can fill an inner void. The void can be filled only from within.

If you have all the trappings of living the good life — a great job, status, and material possessions to name a few — and are still experiencing a fulfillment deficit, it's time to look inside rather than outside. Taoism, like most religions, teaches us that when we look within ourselves, we find all that we need to make our lives happy and fulfilling. By searching within, we achieve clarity and life becomes effortless because we gain simplicity.

In this regard Dr. Martha Friedman stated, "Success based on anything but internal fulfillment is bound to be empty." Indeed, the external world offers only occasional and sporadic pleasures if you don't take time to develop your inner spiritual self. Committing yourself to the inner life and the voice within, on the other hand, results in strength and confidence not available anywhere else.

The inner life can be mysterious. Luckily, this isn't a big problem. The inner life is also wondrous and fascinating. Self-questioning results in self-determination, which leads to much spiritual freedom. Realizing your higher self through your inner world will make you a much more creative and dynamic individual in the outer world. Your life will be a joy to behold because it has richness and quality. You will get to know yourself — and in yourself is the universe.

In short, look inside and you will find more outside. Love yourself while getting to know yourself better. Within yourself is the paradise you have been looking for. Here you will find all the happiness and enlightenment you will ever need.

98

Your Envy Is the Satisfaction and Happiness That You Think Others Are Experiencing

For most of us, the ideal life is the life we do not lead. Indeed, it's the life someone else has. In this regard a French proverb proclaims, "What you can't get is just what suits you." What makes many of us unhappy — even extremely miserable — is our unreasonable and false beliefs about how happy others are. We have some strange idea that most people in Western society are happier than us. Yet this is far from being the case. As Joseph Roux surmised, "I look at what I have not and think myself unhappy; others look at what I have and think me happy."

It's all too easy to fall into the trap of thinking that practically everyone else has a much easier and happier life than you do. There will always be friends, relatives, neighbors, or celebrities who own bigger houses, drive flashier cars, wear more expensive clothes, work at better jobs, or have more physically attractive lovers. How happy they are is another matter. If they are envious of people who have things that they do not have, they certainly aren't happy.

Clearly, one of the most important factors for enjoying life to the fullest is having an absence of envy of others. Your envy, in fact, is the satisfaction and happiness that you think others are experiencing — but aren't. Truth be told, many — perhaps most — of the individuals we envy aren't any happier than we are. Even many of the rich and famous don't deserve our envy. Singer and actress Barbra Streisand revealed, "Oh God, don't envy me, I have my own pains."

To envy the rich and famous is rather ill-considered given that many aren't happy. If you are going to envy anyone, envy the happy poor and the happy disadvantaged of this world. No doubt being happy takes some doing on their part. The core of the matter is that experiencing envy has practically no benefit. Envy is an extremely heavy burden to carry because it breeds contempt and hate. An unknown wise individual once said, "Envy is like acid; it eats away the container that it's in."

No matter how hard you try, you can't be both envious and happy simply because envy is the sidekick of unhappiness. Envy of even one person is a mistake. What's the point of admiring someone else's fortunes so much that you become dissatisfied with your own? Comparing your position with that of others can lead to disillusionment and frustration. You will end up unfairly thinking well of others and disliking yourself.

While you are playing the comparison game, why not play it both ways? Perhaps you would like to live in one of twenty countries, such as Sierra Leone and Afghanistan, where rampant poverty, lack of healthcare, serious malnutrition, constant violence, and perpetual crime contribute to a life expectancy of less than forty-eight years. On this note Helen Keller advised us, "Instead of comparing our lot with that of those who are more fortunate than we are, we should compare it with the lot of the great majority of our fellow men. It then appears we are among the privileged."

The formula for overcoming the envy of others is not all that complex. Relax and count your blessings more often! At least once a week think about the great things your country offers that other countries don't. When you feel deprived because someone has something you don't, keep in mind that billions of people in other countries would gladly trade places with you.

If you haven't been enjoying life lately, gratitude for what you have will do wonders for your well-being. "Just think how happy you would be," an unknown wise person declared, "if you lost everything you have right now, and then got it back." Take the time to appreciate the things you have — your health, your home, your friends, your knowledge, and your creative ability — and you won't have time to be envious of others.

To be happy, you must be grateful for the many things that life has to offer — and there are many if you really look. To identify more of the things for which you should be grateful, adopt this idea from Oprah Winfrey: Keep a gratitude journal. At the end of every day count your blessings and write down at least five wonderful things that happened to you that day. Do this long enough and you will have no psychological need to envy others.

99

If the Grass on the Other Side of the Fence Is Greener, Try Watering Your Side

At some point in our lives we all fall into the trap of believing that the grass is greener on the other side. Whenever you think so, you may want to check it out. Once you get there, you will probably realize that the grass on the other side is pretty much like the grass on your side. What's more, you may even discover that the grass is not green at all.

But if the grass on the other side of the fence is actually greener, try watering your side first. Watering your side is a metaphor for getting your emotional act together and doing something about making your life better. This is about responsibility and commitment. You can sit around and climb imaginary mountains because they aren't there — or you can climb real mountains because they are there. Which do you think will bring you more satisfaction?

Ron Smotherman in his book *Winning Through Enlightenment* concluded: "Satisfaction is for a very select group of people: those who are willing to be satisfied. There aren't many around." If you want to be in the select group of people who are generally satisfied with their lives, you must come to terms with the fact that green grass on your side of the fence — a full, relaxed, satisfying, and happy life, in other words — is the result of commitment and action.

Generally speaking, this is not understood by most humans: We are always free to change our futures by being more alive and creative in the present. Happy, successful people don't expect mysterious forces to make tomorrow worth living. They themselves make it that way by what they do today.

According to the Buddha, "What we think, we become." Therefore, always think and act as if you and your life really matter. At the same time, don't do things because you feel you have to do them. Do things because you want to. The difference in the results you attain will be beyond belief.

It is folly to strive for total comfort, however. Comfort is a double-edged sword. A little will increase health and happiness — too much, and it will destroy both. Thus, be creative, active, and productive by pursuing challenging activities that require a great deal of risk and discomfort.

Have all your goals much bigger than merely making yourself comfortable. A life of passion, purpose, and success is almost always uncomfortable. Pursuing true success entails all aspects of life — the joys and the sorrows, the dullness and the excitement, and the accomplishments and the failures. This will eventually make the grass on your side of the fence a lot greener, which other people will attribute to your good luck.

Luck, incidentally, is the word we often give to remarkable success that someone less privileged and talented than we are has attained. Believe that remarkable success is a result of luck and you will have a lot of lousy luck come your way. Accept that remarkable success is a result of good character and creative action and you will bask in a lot of good luck — and a lot of green grass.

Let go of the notion that everything in life should be easy. If you succeed on the first try, you can be assured that it won't happen again. Either that, or what you have accomplished is not worth boasting about.

Everything keeps its best character by being put to its best use. This applies to both people and things. Thus, pursue goals in harmony with your character and values. Anything short of this and you will be cheating yourself out of many hours of happiness and satisfaction each and every day. Just as telling, there will be no green grass on your side of the fence.

Whatever you dream of doing, begin today. "Twenty years from now you will be more disappointed by the things that you didn't do than by the ones you did do," warned Mark Twain. "So throw off the bowlines. Sail away from the safe harbor. Catch the trade winds in your sails. Explore. Dream. Discover."

100

No Matter How Successful You Become, the Size of Your Funeral Will Still Depend upon the Weather

Perhaps you want to amass a pile of money that would make Warren Buffett and Bill Gates look like paupers. Alternatively, you may be after the Pulitzer, the Nobel, an Oscar, a Tony, a Juno, or an Emmy. No doubt fame and fortune may be yours if you work hard enough. Contrary to popular belief, however, there is less to fame and fortune than first meets the eye.

In our materialistic and celebrity-crazed society it's hard not to think of a happy and successful person as someone who is rich and famous. Fame and fortune are okay in their own ways, but these are not essential ingredients for having lived a full, relaxed, satisfying, and happy life. Few of us derive our greatest joys in life from money, power, or prestige.

To say nothing of the undesirable elements that fame and fortune tend to bring with them. Fred Allen once quipped, "A celebrity is a person who works hard all his life to become well-known, then wears dark glasses to avoid being recognized." Pablo Picasso, with much stronger credentials than I have on the subject of fame and fortune, remarked, "When you are young and without success, you have only a few friends. Then, later on, when you are rich and famous, you still have a few — if you are lucky."

Another dark side of fame and fortune is that by the time you acquire them, you will likely discover they don't bring as many rewards as you originally thought they would. Before you devote your life to becoming rich and famous, it may do you good to ponder this important message from Michael Pritchard: "No matter how rich you become, how famous or powerful, when you die the size of your funeral will still pretty much depend upon the weather." I might add that whether lunch is served can also determine how many people show up at your funeral.

Now, back to being alive. It doesn't matter so much what you do for a living, or how much fame and fortune you attain at what you do, but whether you enjoy peace, health, and love most of the time. If you don't have these, what can replace them? Don't lose sight of the fact that happiness is not a destination, but a journey, a by-product of performing a job well, having good health, doing our duty, pursuing our goals, accepting the inevitable, loving the world, showing gratitude, helping others be happy, and living fully.

Take a close look at the great people of the world. Think Mother Teresa! Think the Dalai Lama! Think Nelson Mandela! Think Mahatma Gandhi! These remarkable individuals lived or live with little material possessions but have experienced happiness, joy, and self-fulfillment throughout their lives. They didn't zealously pursue happiness, joy, and self-fulfillment as goals in themselves. Happiness, joy, and self-fulfillment resulted from a higher purpose, one that involved working toward the common good of humanity.

Live your life like the great people of this world and you will make your stay on Earth as close to a heavenly experience as it can be. Indeed, Zen masters tell us that there is no sense in waiting for Heaven. Zen says that this is life, and today, this is Heaven. Put another way, this is it! Today, this is all you get. Take it or leave it. And you can't leave it. Therefore, make the best of it. This way, in the event you get to Heaven, you will be well-prepared to enjoy yourself there.

The rest of your life begins right now. It can be more than it has ever been. Enjoy everything in life that you can. It is a mistake not to. Let it be a wondrous life. Life is all around you. Live it to its fullest, with all your senses. Listen to it! Look at it! Taste it! Smell it! Feel it!

By all means, spend a good portion of your time attaining the personal success you would like to attain. Ensure, however, that you experience a full, relaxed, satisfying, and happy life along the way. Whatever success means to you, your journey toward it should feel better than the destination. If you are doing what's right for you, it will — regardless of how much fame and fortune you attain.

101

Be Happy While You Are Alive Because You Are A Long Time Dead!

Think about this quietly and carefully: Years from now, as you review your life, what will you regret not having done? Clearly, it won't be to have worked longer and harder at your career. Just as telling, it won't be that you didn't watch more TV.

No doubt you don't want to leave this world with songs unsung that you would like to have sung. Thus, shouldn't you start singing those songs today? Most people go to their graves regretting things they haven't done. The easiest way to become one of them is by joining society's chorus instead of singing your own songs.

Some things are important and some aren't. It's essential that you know how to tell the difference. If your life is a good case study in perpetual stress and turmoil, there's no point in declaring: "I may not be here for a good time, but I'm here for a long time!" What's the point of being here for a long time if you aren't going to enjoy yourself?

Henry David Thoreau warned us: "Oh, God, to reach the point of death and realize you have never lived at all." Instead of wasting your time regretting what you didn't do in your life, use the time to pursue some of them now. Most people who reach sixty-five or beyond look back on their lives in later years with regret. They wish they had set their priorities differently. They wish they hadn't been as concerned about the little things and had spent more time doing the things they had wanted to do.

In a recent survey a number of individuals, all over sixty years old, were asked what advice they would give themselves if they had life to live over. It may do you good to pay attention to the following six of their suggestions: (1) Take the time to find what you really want to do with your life. (2) Take more risks. (3) Lighten up and don't take life so seriously. (4) It's best to suffer from the Peter-Pan syndrome — relive your younger days. What were your dreams when you were young? (5) Be more patient. (6) Live the moment more.

The good news is that it's never too late — or too early, for that matter — to change direction in your life, to be what you might have been. Of course, those who are resistant to change at thirty will be even more resistant to change at ninety-three. Don't be one of them. If you keep doing what you have been doing, you will keep getting what you have been getting well into infinity and beyond.

Some people die at forty-five, but they have experienced a heck of a lot more happiness in those forty-five years than others who have lived to be ninety or one hundred. The reason is that they mastered the moment while they were alive. In this regard, a Scottish proverb advises, "Be happy while you are alive because you are a long time dead."

For independent-minded individuals, freedom contributes to a lot of their happiness. But freedom isn't the ability to do what others are doing. On the contrary, freedom is the ability to do what the majority in society are afraid of doing on their own. Only when you are able to be creative and different — even wildly eccentric — will you be free.

You don't want to end up on your deathbed pleading, "Lord, give me one more shot and I'll give it all I got." As the saying goes, "Get a life." Not just an ordinary life. Get a great life. Get a focused, satisfying, balanced life instead of one filled with nothing but watching TV and other passive activities.

Spare lots of time for family, friends, and leisure. Most important — don't forget to spare time for yourself. Nothing that is human should be foreign to you. Make the small pleasures in life your biggest priorities. Wise people realize that the simple pleasures — nature, health, music, friendship, etc. — are the most satisfying.

Have some perpetual small enjoyment in which you indulge daily. Never miss it, regardless of how busy you are. This will do wonders for your well-being. Indeed, it will do more for your happiness than acquiring the biggest and best of possessions.

Call forth the best you can muster for living life to the fullest regardless of how limited your funds. The Greeks say, "When you are poor, it is important to have a good time." So take the opportunity to drink quality wine or champagne with your friends at least once a week. This is especially important when you have something to celebrate — and even more important when you don't!

Freedom and happiness are easier to attain than you think. Take your lesson from children. Don't fret about the future. Don't regret the past. Live only in the present. The happiness you have at any moment is the only happiness you can ever experience. Reminisce about your great yesterdays, hope for many interesting tomorrows, but, above all, ensure that you live today.

Consider each day you haven't laughed, played, and celebrated your life to be a wasted day. "Keep a green tree in your heart and perhaps the songbird will come," according to a Chinese proverb. You were given three special gifts when you were born: the gifts of life, love, and laughter. Learn to share these gifts with the rest of the world — and the rest of the world will play happily with you.

In the same vein, don't lose touch with the craziness within yourself. Often one gets a reputation for mental stability simply because one doesn't have enough courage to make a fool of oneself. Is it more important to live with zest or to have people think nice things about you? The point is, if you want to be truly alive, forget about what people think.

Always question what your neighbors say or do or think. It is unwise to use the conduct of the majority in society as a viable precedent for your own life. Do so and you will be setting yourself up for much disappointment and disillusionment. What the majority pursue are seldom the things that bring happiness, satisfaction, and freedom to any individual's life.

Resist accepting society's way of living as the right one. Your primary duty is to be yourself. Invent a lifestyle that expresses who you are. In the end, there is no right way of living. There is only your way.

Determine your direction clearly before you choose the speed at which you want to travel. In Western society, most people today are in a hurry to get to places not worth going. Speed in life doesn't count as much as direction. Indeed, where there is no direction, speed doesn't count at all.

To a large degree freedom entails nonattachment to what others can't do without. Zen masters tell us that people become imprisoned by what they are most attached to: Cars. Houses. Money. Egos. Identities. Let go of your attachment to these things and you will be set free.

Give up the idea of a one-way ticket or seven secrets to living happily ever after. The secrets for living a full, rewarding, fulfilled, and enlightened life are not really secrets. These principles have been passed down through the ages but the majority of humans tend to discount them and follow principles that don't work. "In the end these things matter most," revealed Buddha. "How well did you love? How fully did you live? How deeply did you learn to let go?"

When a friend offers to spend time with you either today or tomorrow, always choose today. No individual gets out of this world alive, so the ideal time to live, love, and laugh with your friends is always today. Spending as much time as possible with your friends is solid proof of your intention to live your life now — while you have it — and be dead later — when you are!

It's essential that you identify the resources most important for your present-day happiness. When money is lost, a little is lost. When time is lost, much more is lost. When health is lost, practically everything is gone. And when creative spirit is lost, there is nothing left.

Get the picture? Life is a game in many ways. It is important to play the game here and now, in the present. Find a version of the game worth playing — a version that you truly enjoy. Ensure that you laugh and have fun, even when the score is not in your favor. You have to play the game of life with gusto, and if you get really good at it, you will miraculously transform your world — forever! After all, it's all in how you play the game, isn't it?

Additional
Life Lessons

Life Lesson A-1
Thank Your Mother a Lot While She Is Still Alive

Regardless of their age, the large majority of mothers care for their children in a thousand little ways that their children tend to take for granted. Unfortunately, most of us don't realize how much our mothers mean to us until they are no longer around. Of course, there are many people who truly appreciate their mothers and express their gratitude for them.

"All that I am or ever hope to be," remarked Abraham Lincoln, "I owe to my angel Mother." George Washington declared, "I attribute all my success in life to the moral, intellectual, and physical education which I received from my mother." Jewish people have a proverb about mothers that is even more eloquent: "God could not be everywhere and therefore He made mothers."

Given that my mother passed away while I was in the middle of completing the new edition of this book, allow me to share how I never got to express my love and appreciation for her as much as I would have liked. On the first Sunday of February 2007 I was contemplating whether I should go to a musical performance at our local jazz club. I gave consideration to the fact that on the previous Sunday I had not visited my mother, which I had done virtually every Sunday for almost twenty years. Thus, I decided to skip the musical performance.

I picked up some items from a local supermarket deli and headed over to my mother's apartment. This particular Sunday my sister, Elaine, and her husband, Lorne, also showed up and we had an enjoyable dinner together. Later I noticed that my mother was wheezing after she climbed a flight of stairs. She also complained about how her legs had gotten really stiff lately.

Even so, I would later find out that my mother told her best friend that she had a really great day, because my sister, my brother-in-law, and I had visited her. What's more, earlier in the day, just as my mother was about to call my brother, Kenny, who lives out of the city, he called and talked to her for an hour.

As it turned out, this was the last Sunday dinner that I enjoyed with my mother. You can imagine how fortunate I felt that I had skipped the musical performance. Two days later I called my mother to ask her how she was doing. She complained of severe headaches that wouldn't respond to Tylenol. Later in the evening my sister and her husband drove my mother to the hospital. The doctors decided to keep her for two or three days because of her low oxygen level but they didn't think it was anything serious.

On Wednesday afternoon when I visited my mother at the hospital, I was stunned to find out that the doctors had diagnosed her with acute leukemia. The head doctor indicated that she could live for several weeks — even months — if they gave her blood transfusions and chemo drugs along with morphine. Needless to say, I left the hospital in somewhat of a daze.

That evening I decided that I would visit my mother at least once every day until she passed away. I also decided to get a nice black book in which I would write down all the special things that I wanted to thank her for. I was also going to encourage other people to write in the black book all the things that they liked about my mother.

As fate would have it, the next day my mother took a turn for the worse. The doctor phoned early in the morning and indicated she had only a few days left with her likely losing mental capabilities in a day or two. Soon after I got to the hospital, I decided that I should bring my mother's best friend, Mary Leshchyshyn, to see my mother one last time while she still had her mental capabilities. After I brought Mary to the hospital, she and my mother were able to spend half an hour together while the rest of us went for coffee.

When we got back to my mother's hospital room, I noticed that my mother had gotten worse and was gasping for oxygen. At this point I felt that she might not last more than a day. So I immediately thanked my mother for two or three important things that she had done for me.

She responded — as she struggled for oxygen — by thanking me specifically for having come over every Sunday. (At this point I truly realized how much my weekly Sunday visits meant to her.) I also told my mother that the reason that I had never married was that I had never met a wonderful woman like her.

Shortly after, my mother's best friend, Mary, stated that my mother looked really tired and that she should go home to let my mother rest. My mother was able to say a few more words to Mary including "Don't get what I got." Mary's last words to my mother were "See you later." I would find out soon after from my sister that my mother whispered, "Oh no, you won't." But Mary didn't hear this.

Sadly, while I was driving Mary back to her apartment, my mother passed away. My sister, Elaine, and her husband, Lorne; my cousin, Jerry, and his wife, Lil; and the hospital chaplain, Blaine Allan, were there with her and said a prayer while she passed away. Surprisingly, my mother at eighty-five had her mental capabilities and even a great memory right until her last minutes, given that she was giving instructions to my sister about the funeral, including the dress she wanted to be wearing and how she wanted her head tilted just a bit in the coffin instead of straight up.

I found out a few interesting things shortly after my mother passed away. Blaine, the hospital chaplain, had visited my mother in the early morning and spent about an hour with her. She talked to Blaine about what a great life she had had and how she was sure she was going to pass away that day. Blaine also indicated that my mother was not trying to hang on like some people do.

Later that morning, when my sister arrived, my mother told her, "I'm done." My sister responded, "What are you talking about?" My mother replied, "I lost the stone from my family ring. It's gone so that means that I am gone too." My mother was so sweet and so strong during her last hours. Even the hospital staff talked about the deep affection they had developed for her during her short stay in the hospital.

As hard as my mother's death was on me, there was something remarkably spiritual about it. There were also a few things for which I had to feel grateful. My mother did not have to suffer for a long time like so many people do in their later years. I was thankful that Elaine, Lorne, Jerry, Lil, and Blaine were there with her to say a prayer when she passed away. I also felt relieved that I had brought Mary to the hospital so that she and my mother got to spend half an hour together before my mother left us rather unexpectedly that day.

After I left the hospital that fateful afternoon, I felt blessed that I was able to see my mother her last day and thank her for at least two or three special things that she had done for me. But I was also terribly saddened that I did not get to give her a hundred more reasons why she had meant so much to me. So I wrote a letter to my mother, which follows this photo of her in her twenties:

February 8, 2007

Dear Mom:

I am so saddened that you left us rather suddenly while knowing that in many ways it was the right thing for you to do. I am sorry that I was not there when you passed on but I know that you appreciate that I brought your best friend Mary to see you one last time and I know that Mary appreciated having the chance to see you one last time. Unfortunately, while I was driving Mary back to her home, you left us but Elaine, Lorne, Lil, Jerry, and Blaine were there with you.

I will miss you. I hope that we meet in Heaven. I know that from the way you treated me and the way you treated others — and how much they held you in great esteem and admiration — that you have an outstanding chance of entering Heaven — far greater than me, that's for sure. But I will remember the great things that people loved about you and try to instill as many of your great qualities in myself as I can from now on. Perhaps I will get into Heaven as easily as you.

Because you left rather suddenly, there are so many things that I wanted to thank you for but didn't get a chance. Here are just some of the things I wanted to thank you for:

- Thank you for having stuck by my side so many times and gotten yourself in trouble with Dad when he thought I should be doing something else with my life.
- Thank you for lending me the money to publish my first book although, as you said when I was paying you back, you thought you would never see the money again.
- Thank you for making a prompt decision around eight years ago to sell your house and move into the St Andrew's Retirement Complex — I know that your living in the apartment complex rather than continuing living isolated in the house added several years to your life — and of course joy in other people's lives.
- Thank you for still making the great cabbage rolls this last Christmas that you made all these years even though you had been quite ill just before the holidays.
- Thank you for having taken care of your best friend Mary by buying groceries for her when she couldn't make it out on her own due to her low energy level.
- Thank you for having had the ability to always be so pleasant with everyone that you met.
- Thank you for your appreciation of other people — I can't recall your ever having said a bad word about anyone.

I could go on forever about the things that I would like to thank you for, but I just want to wrap it up by saying I am somewhat mystified — but nevertheless proud of you — for being able to live to the age of eighty-five in generally good health and then make a fairly rapid exit from this planet without having to suffer like so many people do. Great work, Mom!

But I am going to miss you a great deal. Not having the regular Sunday dinners as we have for so many years and not having someone special to phone every day or two are going to be hard on me.

I promise to think of you as I live the rest of my life. I will give much thought every day about the types of things you would have wanted me to do and how you would have liked me to treat other people. I know that this will make me a much better person and I hope that I will have as many great people mourn my passing from this planet as will come to mourn yours.

Thank you, Mom

With all my love
Ernie

I placed this letter under my mother's arm in the coffin when members of my close family and I visited the funeral home to pay our respects the day before the funeral. The next day, after I read a copy of the letter as the eulogy during the funeral service conducted by Father Don Bodnar, a good friend of mine commented that this is the type of letter we should all write to our mothers while they are still living.

To be sure, you should thank your mother a lot for all that she means to you while she is still alive — not only with letters but also with thoughtful comments every time you see her. Clearly, your mother deserves much more than a card, flowers, or candy once a year on Mother's Day. Why not send her a handwritten letter at least once a month? Start today because you never know when she may lose her life suddenly.

Here are a few words from Washington Irving to remind us a little more about how important mothers are to us: "A mother is the truest friend we have, when trials heavy and sudden, fall upon us; when adversity takes the place of prosperity; when friends who rejoice with us in our sunshine desert us; when trouble thickens around us, still will she cling to us, and endeavor by her kind precepts and counsels to dissipate the clouds of darkness, and cause peace to return to our hearts."

I was fortunate that I saw my mother fifteen to twenty minutes before she passed away and was able to at least thank her for a few things. I am also blessed that I get to dedicate this book to her and will have her name live on at least in some small spiritual way due to me — and, of course, due to the great person that she was. You may not get these same opportunities. So again, thank your mother a lot while she is still alive. Trust me — you will deeply regret it later if you don't.

Life Lesson A-2
Flowers, Cards, and Candy Are Not the Essence of Mother's Day

As much as I loved my mother, it will come as a surprise to some people that over the years I didn't buy her flowers, cards, or candy for Mother's Day. I did buy her dinner, however, and spent quality time with her every Mother's Day. Perhaps you should do likewise.

Truth be known, you don't have to feel guilty about not buying gifts to help your mother celebrate Mother's Day. Not buying your mother cards, flowers, or candy to help her celebrate this special event is not about being stingy and saving yourself a few bucks, however. There is a much better reason. We have to go back to the origins of Mother's Day to place this matter in proper perspective.

Anna May Jarvis was just two weeks shy of forty-two, working for a life insurance company in Philadelphia, when her mother (Mrs. Anna Reese Jarvis) died on May 9, 1905. It was the second Sunday of the month. The next year Anna May Jarvis made her life goal to see her mother and motherhood honored annually throughout the world. Jarvis felt children often neglected to appreciate their mother enough while she was still alive. She hoped Mother's Day would increase respect for parents and strengthen family bonds.

Two years after her mother's death, Anna Jarvis and her friends began a letter-writing campaign to gain the support of influential ministers, businessmen, and congressmen in declaring a national Mother's Day holiday. In 1914, President Woodrow Wilson signed a proclamation from the U.S. Congress to establish the second Sunday in May as Mother's Day forevermore.

Ironically, the commercialization of the day she had founded in honor of motherhood — today it is the biggest business day of the year for U.S. restaurants and flower shops — was not what Anna May Jarvis had envisioned. Jarvis wanted people to spend a lot of quality time with their mothers and let their mothers know how special they were.

Sadly, Jarvis, who never married and was never a mother herself, retired from her job at the insurance company to spend her remaining thirty-four years, and her entire fortune of over $100,000, campaigning against the commercialization of Mother's Day.

Whenever she could, Anna May Jarvis would speak out. She was known to crash florists' conventions to express her distaste for their "profiteering" from Mother's Day. Eventually too old to continue her campaign, she ended up deaf and blind — not to mention penniless — in a West Chester, Pennsylvania, sanitarium, where she died in November 1948 at the age of eighty-four.

"Why not give your mother flowers, cards, or candy?" you may ask. "Flowers," declared Jarvis, "are about half dead by the time they're delivered." As for candy, Jarvis advised, "Mother's Day has nothing to do with candy. Candy is junk. You give your mother a box of candy and then go home and eat most of it yourself."

"Well, then what's wrong with cards?" you may add. Jarvis felt that "a maudlin, insincere printed card or a ready-made telegram means nothing except that you're too lazy to write to the woman who has done more for you than anyone else in the world."

Tell your mother the truth about Mother's Day and you won't have to spend money on flowers, candy, and cards to help her celebrate her special event of the year. Heck, you don't even have to buy her a copy of this book as a gift. You should, however, make her dinner or take her out to a fine restaurant.

Most important, you should spend a lot of quality time with her. Your mother will appreciate this immensely. What's more, if she were still living today, Anna May Jarvis would be so pleased that you celebrate the second Sunday of May with your mother in the true spirit and essence of Mother's Day!

Life Lesson A-3
Fortune Resides on the Other Side of Fear

How many opportunities in life have you missed due to unreasonable fears about how things will turn out? Most of us, in fact, have missed many. The problem with fear is that it doesn't know how to distinguish real dangers from imaginary ones. Fear, above all else, prevents most of us from living our dreams.

Unfortunately, there is a lot of support in our society for fearful thinking. When you have a promising idea for a new product, new service, or unconventional business, you won't have any trouble at all in finding people who are critical of your idea, find fault with it, or focus on its negative aspects. The more attention you pay to these people, the more fear you will experience.

The only way to conquer any fear is to confront it head-on. Clearly, our main fear is that we will fail. Foremost on our minds is the humiliation of failure. In other words, no one likes to look like a loser. Once you realize that failure and success are two sides of the same coin, you will have a lot more success in your life.

It may come as a surprise to fearful people who never attempt anything daring that most individuals who have had a great measure of success in their lives still experience the fear of failure. Take, for example, Bruce McCall, who, above all, considers himself a humorist. McCall, also an illustrator and author, has attained a good measure of success as a writer, given that he has had over 200 pieces published in *The New Yorker*.

Even so, McCall still submits all his work on spec and admitted to a reporter with *The Globe and Mail* that he is surprised when a project is accepted. McCall, it would seem, is one of those able individuals, like millions of us, who underestimates his own creative ability.

The point is, we all have our doubts and our fears about our projects and career aspirations — even if we already have had great success in our field of endeavor. The most successful of us don't use these fears and doubts to stop us, however. Instead, we keep on going in spite of our doubts and fears. If you would like to be successful in your personal way as Bruce McCall has been in his personal way, your willingness to confront fear is crucial.

If you want to move to another level in your life, you have to learn how to be terribly uncomfortable while you experience your fear. The only way to conquer fear is to experience it while actually doing whatever you fear. Fear without action keeps your life small. Fortune, truth be known, resides on the other side of fear.

Lest you think that you can totally eliminate the fear of failure forever after being a major success in your field, perish the thought. You will always experience some fear when there is risk involved. Even though I have spent many years reprogramming myself and learning as much as I can about what it takes to be successful in my own way, I still experience the fear of failure when I undertake a new project. Self-publishing this book, for example, has resulted in my experiencing the fear of failure even though I have had a fair measure of success in the past few years with my books.

The core of the matter is that individuals who achieve creative success are willing to confront their fears and take risks that others — even the experts — won't. How many times have you read about a person who took a chance with an idea, encountered some real obstacles, and made it to the top? How many times have you had the following thought? "Wow, look at what she accomplished! I wish I had the courage and commitment to have done that, given that I have come up with many promising ideas."

No doubt you have generated at least a few creative ideas that have great potential in the marketplace. I believe it was American historian Will Durant who stated that in every work of genius we recognize our own discarded ideas. No matter how gifted you are, you will have to experiment with different ideas if you want one to click. Most important, you will have to confront your fear of failure, and test the ideas. Bold, creative effort will dispel your fears and eventually bring you good fortune.

Life Lesson A-4
Forget How Old You Are — This Becomes More Important the Older You Get

Age, you will be happy to hear, is not all it's made out to be. It's how you look at it that counts most. "He who is of a calm and happy nature will hardly feel the pressure of age," the Greek philosopher Plato told us, "but to him who is of an opposite disposition youth and age are equally a burden."

After all these years, experts are still proving that Plato was right. In a recent study reported in the *Journal of Personality and Social Psychology*, researchers claim that elderly people can actually think themselves into the grave a lot faster than they would prefer. Indeed, people with negative views about aging shorten their lives by 7.6 years as compared to their counterparts who have a more positive view of life.

Surprisingly, a positive view about aging can have a greater effect than good physical health. The researchers, led by psychologist Becca Levy of Yale University, reported, "The effect of more positive self-perceptions of aging on survival is greater than the physiological measures of low systolic blood pressure and cholesterol, each of which is associated with a longer lifespan of four years or less."

"Our study carries two messages," concluded the researchers. "The discouraging one is that negative self-perceptions can diminish life expectancy. The encouraging one is that positive self-perceptions can prolong life expectancy." The lesson here is that you shouldn't waste too much time and energy worrying about getting older. "Never think oldish thoughts," advised James A. Farley. "It's oldish thoughts that make a person old."

Talk to active elderly people with a *joie de vivre* and you will learn that they are young at heart and don't perceive themselves as old. Sure, they realize that they are physically limited to some degree, but psychologically they don't see age having much to do with their true selves. This applies whether they are in their sixties or nineties.

As a matter of course many upbeat retirees usually feel extremely uncomfortable when in the presence of people their own age, primarily because the majority of people their age think and act old. Simply put, active and happy elderly people don't want to waste their retirement years listening to people their own age complain about the problems of being old.

"There is a fountain of youth," declared Sophia Loren. "It is your mind, your talents, the creativity you bring to your life, and the lives of the people you love. When you learn to tap this source, you will have truly defeated age."

By virtue of their positive thinking, many happy and active seniors have expanded the concept of middle age into the seventh decade. According to a 2002 study by The National Council on the Aging (NCOA), in this day and age one-third of Americans in their seventies consider themselves middle-aged. Among respondents age sixty-five to sixty-nine, nearly half (45 percent) said they considered themselves middle-aged.

Pablo Picasso said, "Age only matters when one is aging. Now that I have arrived at a great age, I might just as well be twenty." Thinking young can help you to stay busily and happily involved in your later years. Somerset Maugham wrote his last book at eighty-four. Giuseppe Verdi was still composing operas in his eighties. Leopold Stokowski founded the American Symphony Orchestra at eighty and recorded twenty albums in his nineties. At ninety-six, Stokowski — an eternal optimist no doubt — signed a six-year recording contract.

These people appear to be somewhat remarkable, and in a way they are. They are not unusual, however. Hundreds of thousands of people in their seventies, eighties, and nineties have an incredible zest for life and show great vigor, enthusiasm, and physical ability for living. Like these active and happy individuals, you shouldn't let how old you are dictate when you enter old age. Indeed, one of the secrets to happiness is to forget how old you are — this becomes more important the older you get.

Life Lesson A-5
Flat Out — Great Friends Rock!

Not surprisingly, friendship figures at the top of most everyone's list when researchers ask, "What gives meaning to your life?" It follows that friendship is truly one of the best gifts we can give ourselves. Legendary jazz vocalist Billie Holiday once said, "If I don't have friends, then I ain't nothing."

Great friends enrich our minds, inspire our imaginations, and enlighten our spirits. To be happy, we require friends in our lives because we have needs. It's rather tricky — probably impossible — for us as individuals to fulfill all our needs by ourselves. One friend may satisfy a certain need and another friend may satisfy a different need.

The key to winning the friendship game is having real friends — and not merely companions. For a friendship to succeed, however, it must work both ways in all respects. You must trust your friends, and they must trust you. You must be getting something of value from them, and they must be receiving something of equal value from you. You must find them pleasant to be around, and they must find you just as pleasant.

One neat thing is that you can have many types of friends: Male friends. Female friends. Casual friends. Good friends. Great friends. You can have different friends for different reasons and different occasions. Best of all, you can have one person whom you consider your overall best friend.

The fascinating thing about friends is that you get to choose them, unlike relatives whom you have to endure at family gatherings, or colleagues with whom you have to share space in a workplace. Another great thing about friends is that you can dump them much easier than relatives or work colleagues when you no longer want them around.

Of course, people get to choose you as a friend — and they can dump you pretty fast if they no longer want you around. After all, the friendship game is full of surprises — some remarkably pleasant and some not all that pleasant.

While it may appear accidental, it's possible to dramatically increase the chances of meeting a new friend or two — and keeping them as friends forever.

This is the really cool part: Once you understand the fundamentals of friendship, you may never have to be without any true friends. Ever again! Best of all, real friends will support you in your pursuit of your personal goals and ambitions much more than colleagues that you encounter in a typical workplace or acquaintances that you casually meet in a pub.

Real success in life means that you have a lot of time to spend with your friends — and are in fact doing so. This leads to an important reminder: If you are working hard to attain whatever success means to you, but don't have time to make any real friends, or spend time with ones you already have, you haven't attained real success! After all, isn't having great times with great friends what a great life is ultimately all about?

All things considered, great friends make life complete. Have you ever noticed that when you have dinner at a restaurant with a good friend, a mediocre meal will end up tasting like gourmet? Good friends will also make a long journey seem a lot shorter. They will be there to make you feel better if you get into a fight with a spouse, colleague, or relative. Best of all, even ten minutes in the company of a good friend will make any lousy day worth living. Ultimately, great friendship doubles your joys and expels most of your sorrows.

At this time it is worth remembering one of the most important aspects of friendship: With a real friend by your side, nothing is ever so good that it can't get better. This is what makes the difficult task of nurturing great friends so worthwhile. The truth is that you may go broke, become divorced, and get fired — but as long as you have real friends to spend time with, you still have life and happiness. Indeed, best friends are the most important ingredient in the recipe for having a full, relaxed, satisfying, and happy life.

EPILOGUE: Pets. Spouses. Kids. These are all worth having. Even careers, money, and possessions are okay in their own ways. But, flat out — great friends rock!

About the Author

Ernie J. Zelinski is a leading authority on early retirement and solo-entrepreneurship. His recent works include the career book *Real Success Without a Real Job*, the bestseller *How to Retire Happy, Wild, and Free* (over 77,000 copies sold and published in seven foreign languages), and the international bestseller *The Joy of Not Working* (over 210,000 copies sold and published in

Photograph by Greg Gazin

seventeen languages). Ernie has negotiated ninety book deals with publishers in twenty-four countries for his fifteen books.

Ernie has an Engineering degree and an MBA from the University of Alberta. Feature articles about Ernie and his books have appeared in major newspapers including *USA TODAY*, *Oakland Tribune*, *Boston Herald*, *The Washington Post*, *Toronto Star*, and *Vancouver Sun*.

You can send an e-mail to Ernie at vip-books@telus.net or write to him at:

> Visions International Publishing
> P.O. Box 4072
> Edmonton AB
> Canada   T6E 4S8

To download a free e-book with over half of Ernie's international bestseller *How to Retire Happy, Wild, and Free: Retirement Wisdom That You Won't Get from Your Financial Advisor* — or check out his latest projects including *The 437 Best Things Ever Said about Retirement* and *The 787 Best Things Ever Said about Money* — visit his funky websites:

> www.retirement-wisdom.com
>
> www.real-success.ca
>
> www.thejoyofnotworking.com